'A Mighty Fortress of God'

The Siege of Münster 1534-35

Doug Miller

Helion & Company Limited
Unit 8 Amherst Business Centre
Budbrooke Road
Warwick
CV34 5WE
England
Tel. 01926 499 619
Email: info@helion.co.uk
Website: www.helion.co.uk
X, formerly Twitter: @helionbooks
Visit our blog https://helionbooks.wordpress.com/

Published by Helion & Company 2024
Designed and typeset by Mary Woolley, Battlefield Design (www.battlefield-design.co.uk)
Cover designed by Paul Hewitt, Battlefield Design (www.battlefield-design.co.uk)

Text © Douglas Miller 2024
Photographs and illustrations © as individually credited
Colour artwork by Giorgio Albertini © Helion & Company 2024
Maps by George Anderson © Helion & Company 2024

Every reasonable effort has been made to trace copyright holders and to obtain their permission for the use of copyright material. The author and publisher apologise for any errors or omissions in this work and would be grateful if notified of any corrections that should be incorporated in future reprints or editions of this book.

ISBN 978-1-804515-55-6

British Library Cataloguing-in-Publication Data.
A catalogue record for this book is available from the British Library.

All rights reserved. No part of this publication may be reproduced, stored in a retrieval system, or transmitted, in any form, or by any means, electronic, mechanical, photocopying, recording or otherwise, without the express written consent of Helion & Company Limited.

For details of other military history titles published by Helion & Company Limited contact the above address or visit our website: http://www.helion.co.uk.

We always welcome receiving book proposals from prospective authors.

Contents

Chronology		iii
Acknowledgements		v
Preface		vii
1	The Rise of Anabaptism and the Causes of the Siege	13
2	A Mighty Fortress –The Fortification of Münster	23
3	The Bishop's Siege preparations	32
4	Initial Siege Efforts 1534	49
5	The Defence of the City 1534	64
6	The Erection of the Blockhouses	82
7	The Defence of the City 1535	89
8	The Final Assault	96
9	Aftermath	108
10	Conclusion	116
Colour Plate Commentaries		118
Appendices:		
I	The Bishop's Articles of War	124
II	The first Ordinance introduced by the twelve elders for the political government in the city of Münster	125
III	List of officers of the court as decreed by Jan von Leiden	129
IV	The Costs of the Siege	135
V	Glossary of Fortification Terms	137
Bibliography		139

Chronology

1525

17 January	First adult baptism in Zurich
	Münster wins independence from Church and installs a degree of self-rule with government by the city council and mayor

1529

23 April	Emperor Karl V (Charles V) orders wholesale extermination of 'every Anabaptist and rebaptised man and woman of the age of reason' by Imperial decree

1532

February	Prominent citizens meet to organize resistance to the Bishop, mob attacks Catholic churches
March	New Prince-Bishop, Franz von Waldeck, assumes post. City limits Catholic freedom of worship and assembly

1533

June	Melchior Hoffman, peaceful Anabaptist leader, imprisoned in Strasbourg; Jan Matthijs, Dutch convert, assumes leadership and advocates militancy
June-Sept	Influx of foreigners destabilizes Münster

1534

5 January	Anabaptist self-declared prophet Jan Matthijs identifies Münster as the "New Jerusalem" and several of his disciples from the Low Countries, including the tailor from Leiden known as John Bockelson (aka Jan van Leiden) enter the city
10 February	Bernd Knipperdolling, the Mayor, 'officially' declares the city's opposition to the Catholic Prince Bishop of Münster, Franz von Waldeck

'A MIGHTY FORTRESS OF GOD': THE SIEGE OF MÜNSTER 1534-35

27 February	Bishop lays siege to the city
5 April	(Easter Sunday) Jan Matthijs leads a sortie from the city and is brutally killed by the bishop's landsknechts
25 May	First assault by the bishop's troops on Whit Monday ends in failure
16 June	Failed attempt to assassinate the Bishop by Hille Feicken
25 August	Delegation enters the city to discuss surrender terms
27 August	Bombardment of city begins
31 August	Second unsuccessful assault
1 September	Official coronation of Jan van Leiden as 'King of New Israel'
	Commencement of the construction of the blockhouses
23 October	Anabaptist 'apostles' are sent to neighbouring cities to drum up support
2 November	Council of war decides to starve the city into submission. The Bishop's emissary Fabricius is sent into the city to negotiate peace terms but is unsuccessful

1535

March	Starvation in the city begins to take effect. Old and frail are released into Bishop's camps
April-May	Exodus continues and includes two defectors, Henry Gresbeck and Hans van der Langenstraat, who reveal a plan to mount a night assault
24/25 June	Final assault. Münster is retaken

1536

22 January	Jan of Leiden, Bernhard Knipperdolling, and Bernhard Krechting are tortured and executed in the marketplace of Münster

Acknowledgements

The following individuals have helped me with the preparation of this book. Thanks must go to Dr Ralf Klötzel, Dr Bernd Thier, Christopher Mackay, and Henning Stoffers for helping me orientate events with specific locations in the city today and the clarification of some finer points. Thanks are also due to Jane Malcom-Davies and the staff at 'the Tudor Tailor' for their assistance on aspects of the court costume of Jan van Leiden. Geoff Laws assisted me with sketches and matters graphical and special thanks to Andy Drummond for reading my drafts and to Professor Lyndal Roper for photographing artefacts and buildings in Münster. Finally thanks are due to Ursula Grimm, Sabine Ahlbrand-Dornseif and Hanna Neander at the LWL-Museum für Kunst und Kultur, Westfälisches Landesmuseum, Münster for their assistance with contemporary woodcuts of the siege.

Preface

> A mighty Fortress is our God,
> A Bulwark never failing;
> Our Helper He amid the flood
> Of mortal ills prevailing:
> For still our ancient foe
> Doth seek to work us woe;
> His craft and power are great,
> And, armed with cruel hate,
> On earth is not his equal.
> (Martin Luther: verse 1 of *A Mighty Fortress Is Our God*)[1]

In the years immediately following the crushing defeat by the princes' mercenary armies of the insurgency known as the German Peasants' War,[2] Martin Luther penned one of his best-known hymns, perhaps safe in the knowledge that his 'church' could no longer be threatened by the common people. Whilst his Reformation continued to drive a wedge through The Holy Roman Empire, Luther had kept his faith in a church-state maintained by the princes. Many of his more radical reformist preacher contemporaries, however, had challenged the existing status quo – foremost among them Thomas Müntzer[3] – who had rallied the peasants at the 'battle' of Frankenhausen in 1525 for religious and civil liberty.[4]

Although Müntzer had been openly hostile to the authorities, seeing them very much as part of the problem, other reformist preachers were mounting a much more fundamental challenge to both the Catholic and Protestant orthodoxy in their propagation of adult baptism. Many of these preachers had been present at Frankenhausen[5] and in the years following

---

1   *Ein feste Burg Istunser Gott* is one of the best-known hymns by Martin Luther, composed sometime between 1527 and 1529.
2   D. Miller, *The German Peasants' War 1524-6*, (Warwick: Helion & Co., 2023).
3   A. Drummond, *The Dreadful History and Judgement of God on Thomas Müntzer*, (London and New York: Verso, 2024).
4   D. Miller, *Frankenhausen 1525*, (Seaton Burn: Blagdon Publishing, 2017).
5   James Stayer, *The German Peasants' War and the Anabaptist Community of Goods*, (Montreal: McGill Queen's University Press 1991) p.83.

the Peasants' War, the rejection of infant baptism in favour of rebaptism of the 'Elect' into the house of God spread out from Switzerland and Saxony attracting thousands of followers in spite of the cruellest repression. Undeterred, the practice of adult baptism continued to spread southwards to Franconia and Bavaria, Austria and the Tyrol, before extending further eastwards into Moravia and Hungary. Eventually the movement, Anabaptism, established 'pockets' along the length of the Rhine, before putting down firm roots in the Netherlands. From established bases in the Low Countries, Anabaptism spread over into northern Germany, where it founded the remarkable 'Kingdom of Münster' of 1534–1535.

It was here that a large religious community came together, protected in their own 'mighty fortress of God' quite different from Luther's ideal, and which proved strong enough to withstand a siege for almost sixteen months. This book seeks to provide some insight into how the city was able to repel the siege army of the Catholic Bishop Franz von Waldeck for such a length of time. Whilst explanations are to be found in the methods of fortification and siegeworks and the tactics employed to utilise the same in the early modern era, and the problems of financing and marshalling a siege army of landsknecht mercenaries, the actions of key individuals were decisive in the defence and ultimate capitulation of the 'New Jerusalem'.

Thanks to many documents, eyewitness accounts, correspondence, and minutes of meetings, we can get a detailed insight into the siege. Texts from four principal sources have been used for this book. A key basis for information and narrative details since the mid-nineteenth century has been the 1853 collection of eyewitness accounts of the Anabaptist Kingdom of Münster complete with a full introduction and commentary provided by C. A. Cornelius in *Witness Reports Concerning the Anabaptist Kingdom in Münster*.[6] This work includes the influential extensive eyewitness account of the carpenter Heinrich Gresbeck, a formerly enthusiastic Anabaptist who experienced the entire Münster rebellion before escaping to betray his fellow citizens to Bishop von Waldeck by providing him with the means to mount a decisive night assault that resulted in the capitulation of the city. The most detailed and best-known source is the extensive *Narratiohistorica Anabaptisticifuroris Monasterium* by Hermann Kerssenbroch. This account was, however, not completed until 1575. Born in 1520, Kerssenbroch was 13 when his family was banished from the city. He did not return until 1550, and then it was to serve as Rector of the Cathedral school, and he began his history of the uprising in 1566. Using a rich source of material at hand, including his own memories as a boy and eyewitness statements of his contemporaries, as well as his intimate knowledge of the city, his account has been particularly useful in creating a picture of the fortifications of the citadel, in detailing of the Bishop's siege efforts as well as the efforts on the part of the Anabaptists to repel their attackers. Thanks to the English

---

6   C. A. Cornelius *Berichte der Augenzeugen über das Münsterische Wiedertauferreich* (Münster: Theisssing'schen Buchhandlungsverlag 1853).

translations with explanatory notes undertaken by Christopher Mackay of both these texts, we have access to the rich but sometimes contradictory detail provided in what are, essentially, partisan accounts, biased towards the authorities.[7] Whilst the accuracy of Kerssenbroch's version of events has attracted criticism from a number of historians, his description of Münster's fortifications is nevertheless highly detailed and indeed proved far too revealing for the defence minded city council when it was published.[8]

In addition, of particular importance are the writings and letters of Bernhard Rothmann, the main theologian and preacher of the Anabaptists in Münster, as well as the correspondence of the besiegers, eyewitness accounts of visitors to Münster and the confessions and interrogation protocols of the main Anabaptist protagonists Jan van Leiden, Bernd Knipperdolling, and Bernd Krechting. These provide insight into the behaviour of the Anabaptist leadership as events unfolded within the city walls during the siege.[9]

Finally, of particular use in helping to structure the chapters of this book, has been by far the most authoritative account of the siege and conquest of the city undertaken by Karl Heinz Kirchhoff,[10] who has made extensive use of a wide range of archive material, including the siege accounts ledgers kept by the Paymaster (*Pfennigmeister*), Johannes Hageboke.[11]

Whilst often these accounts need to be critically assessed from a historiographical point of view, since historians have generally approached the Anabaptist Kingdom with a hostile or dismissive attitude, interpreting this episode as a 'debacle' or 'catastrophe' with its principal actors frequently judged as 'fanatical', they nevertheless provide us with a detailed factual insight into the ways in which sieges, and their defence, were undertaken in the Early Modern Era.

---

7 *Meister Heinrich Gresbeck Bericht von der Wiedertaufe in Münster* is available in English with a commentary by Christopher S. Mackay, False *Prophets and Preachers, Henry Gresbeck's Account of the Anabaptist Kingdom of Münster* (Kirksville: Truman State University Press 2016). Hermann von Kerssenbroch, (Christopher S. Mackay tr.), *Narratio Historica Anabaptistici Furoris Monasterium,* (*Narrative of the Anabaptist Madness. The overthrow of Münster, the Famous Metropolis of Westphalia*) (Leiden–Boston: Brill 2007)

8 Christopher Mackay, *False Prophets & Preachers: Henry Gresbeck's Account of the Anabaptist Kingdom of Münster*, (Kirksville: Truman State University Press, 2016), footnote p.97.

9 Richard Von Dülmen, *Das Tauferreich zu* Münster *1534-5 Dokumente*, (Munich: Deutscher Taschenbuchverlag, 1974).

10 Karl Heinz Kirchoff, 'Die Belagerung und Eroberung Münsters 1534-5' in *Westfälische Zeitschrift*, vol. 112 (1962), pp.77-170. www.lwl.org/westfaelische-geschichte/txt/wz-5790.pdf (accessed 4 July 2023).

11 Ernst Müller (ed.), Die Abrechnung des Johannes Hageboke über die Kosten der Belagerung der Stadt Münster 1534-1535 Nebst der Abrechnung des Heinrich Flyncterinck über Büchsenmeister, Artillerie u. a. in *Veröffentlichungen der Historischen Kommission des Provinzialinstituts für Westfälische Landes- und Volkskunde III*, (Münster: Aschendorffsche Verlagsbuchhandlung 1937).

The structure of the book is as follows. Chapter 1 contextualises Bishop Franz von Waldeck's siege of Münster against the rise of Anabaptism and its particular trajectory within the city. Chapter 2 deals with the way in which the old walled cathedral city had developed into a mighty fortress by the time of the onset of the siege in 1534. Developments in siege warfare which informed the steps taken by the Bishop during the early phase of the blockade are covered in Chapter 3, while Chapter 4 details the failed efforts during the first year of the siege. Chapter 5 focuses on the successful efforts by the Anabaptists to repel the Bishop's initial assaults in the first year prompting the decision to starve the city into submission through the erection of a ring of blockhouses – the subject of Chapter 6. Chapter 7 concerns itself with events inside the beleaguered city as the siege moved into its second year, while Chapter 8 details the plans to mount a night assault on the city and the subsequent street fighting inside the citadel leading to the capitulation of the defenders. The final Chapter deals with the aftermath and the executions of the city's leaders. Much of the narrative consists of excerpts and quotes from the Mackay translations. Please note, for clarity, footnotes and page references to these eyewitness accounts use the names Gresbeck and Kerssenbroch rather than the translator. In addition to paraphrased translations from the Kirchhoff texts, some new translations have been necessary for which I accept full responsibility for any inaccuracies which may have emerged in the process. Similarly every effort has been made to provide the correct attribution to the images contained within the book.

A note re titles and towns: throughout I have used the German form of the names of towns and locations, similarly I have used the German titles of rank with the exception of Bishop/Prince-Bishop, Elector and Emperor, the use of which is so commonplace as to create a confusion if the German form was used – perhaps especially so in the term *Kaiser* which has underlying echoes in English.

Doug Miller,
Newcastle, May 2024

1

The Rise of Anabaptism and the Causes of the Siege

Chronology

805	Bishopric of Münster is founded
1517	Martin Luther's 95 theses herald the Protestant Reformation
1523	In Zurich, Switzerland where Protestantism has taken hold, Conrad Grebel and Felix Mantz take a more radical stance denying the validity of infant baptism

1525

21 January	The Zurich council forbids Conrad Grebel and Felix Mantz from disseminating their views. In defiance the first adult baptisms take place
1524–1525	German Peasants' War – numerous Anabaptists are involved in and/or inspired by events
1525–1526	Guildsmen and Mayor of the Council of Münster declare independence from the Catholic Church
1526	Adult baptism is outlawed in Switzerland. Movement disperses throughout Western Europe
1527	Schleitheim Confession condemning the Catholic Church, infant baptism, oaths, celibacy, and transubstantiation[1]
1529	Emperor Karl V orders the extermination of every rebaptised man and woman 'of the age of reason'

---

[1] Offering bread and wine are changed into the body and blood of Christ.

1530

April	Melchior Hoffman is rebaptised and then spreads the idea of adult rebaptism in Strasbourg
1530/31	Bernhard Rothmann, an anti-Catholic cleric, begins to preach in St Mauritz church, Münster

1533

February	Münster becomes officially Lutheran
June-July	Rothmann is convinced by Melchior Hoffman to withdraw from Lutheranism and support the principle that adults must be rebaptised
	Bernd Rothmann is politically supported by the new mayor of Münster Bernd Knipperdolling

1534

5 January	Anabaptist self-declared prophet Jan Matthijs identifies Münster as the 'New Jerusalem' and several of his disciples from the Low Countries, including the tailor from Leiden known as John Bockelson, enter the city
10 February	Knipperdolling officially declares the city's opposition to the Catholic Prince Bishop of Münster, Franz von Waldeck
27 February	Bishop von Waldeck lays siege to the city

On 17 January 1525, the year in which vast tracts of Southern and Central Germany became embroiled in the popular uprising known as the Peasants' War, a Swiss reformist preacher by the name of Conrad Grebel performed the first adult baptism in Zurich. This harmless, indeed most sensible act described by some as the most revolutionary act of the Reformation,[2] was to provoke the opprobrium of the Catholic and Lutheran churches alike, leading to the most vicious repression of this newly emerging religious sect. Pejoratively referred to as rebaptisers, because followers committed to a second baptism, the 'Ana'-baptists believed that infants and young children were not accountable for sin until they could exercise repentance of their own free will and publicly commit to their faith through adult baptism. For Anabaptists the church had to be separated from the state and they refused to swear oaths, including those to civil authorities, which they believed existed only for the punishment of sinners.

Since the rejection of infant baptism presented an open challenge to the existing political order by breaking the lifelong acceptance of the authority of the established church, whether Catholic or Lutheran, Anabaptists posed

---

[2] William E. Juhnke, 'Anabaptism and Mormonism: a Study in Comparative History' in *The John Whitmer Historical Association Journal*, volume 2 (1982), pp.38–46.

THE RISE OF ANABAPTISM AND THE CAUSES OF THE SIEGE

a serious threat to the political order. This brought the whole weight of the Holy Roman Empire church state upon their heads. On 4 January 1528, Emperor Karl V "protector of the most holy Christian faith", mandated that each and every Anabaptist and rebaptised person, man or woman of accountable age, shall be brought from natural life to death with fire and sword and the like". A charge which was elevated to an imperial law – the so-called Anabaptist mandate of 23 April 1529 – and reaffirmed a year later by the consent of the assembled Imperial Estates at the Diet of Augsburg.[3] The respective sovereigns and the Roman Catholic Church, the Lutheran and Reformed clergy were thus legitimised in their persecution of the Anabaptists which involved the seizure of property, exile, torture, slavery, and punishment by execution. The executions were to run into thousands.[4]

1.1. The public execution of Maria van Beckum. (Engraving by Jan Luckyen 1544. Courtesy of Rijksmuseum, Amsterdam)

---

3   This was enunciated at the Augsburg Confession convened in 1530 by Karl V who called on the Princes and Free Territories in Germany to explain their religious convictions to restore religious and political unity in the Holy Roman Empire. P. Melanchthon, The Augsburg Confession, Articles V and IX, 1530. The full text is at https://en.wikisource.org/wiki/Augsburg_Confession (accessed 31 March 2020).

4   The martyrdom of Anabaptists has been well chronicled https://de.wikipedia.org/wiki/M%C3%A4rtyrer_der_T%C3%A4uferbewegung

'A MIGHTY FORTRESS OF GOD': THE SIEGE OF MÜNSTER 1534-35

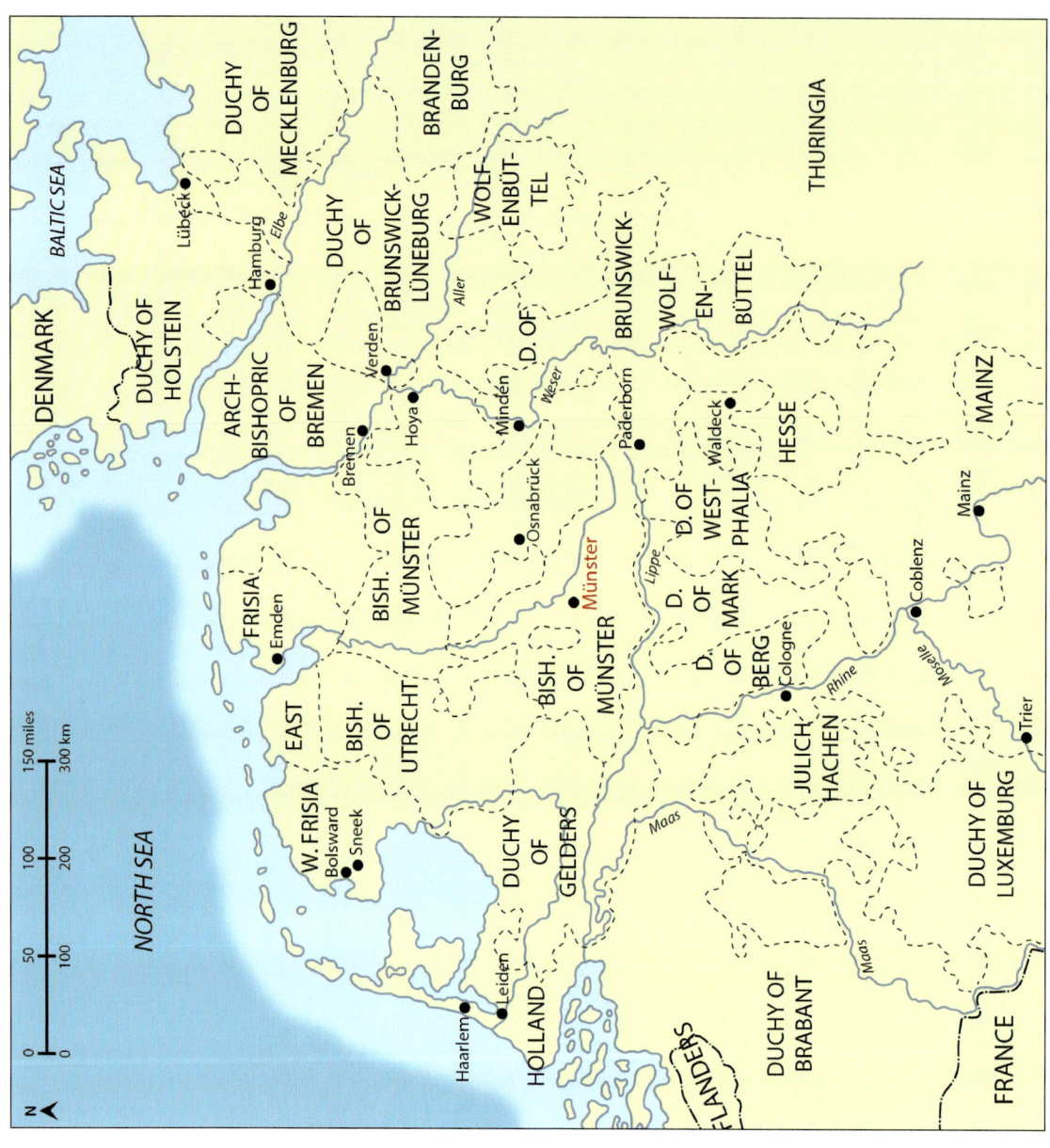

M.1.1. The Lower Rhenish-Westphalian Circle was an Imperial Circle of the Holy Roman Empire. It comprised territories of the former Duchy of Lower Lothringia, Frisia and the Westphalian part of the former Duchy of Saxony. The circle was made up of numerous small states, Imperial cities, lordships, duchies, counties, and prince bishoprics. The Circle's largest ecclesiastical territory was held by the Prince-Bishop of Münster. Münster was bordered by The United Provinces to the west, by Cleves, West Recklinghausen, and Mark in the south, Paderborn and Osnabrück in the east. In the north and north-east it bordered East Frisia, Oldenburg, and the Electorate of Hanover (est. 1692). The territory of the Diocese of Münster originally created in the year 795 was bounded on the west, south, and north-west by the dioceses of Cologne and Utrecht, on the east and north-east by Osnabrück. The diocese also included districts remote from the bulk of its territory, namely, the five Frisian districts on the lower Ems (Hugmerki, Hunusgau, Fivelgau, Federitgau, and Emsgau).

THE RISE OF ANABAPTISM AND THE CAUSES OF THE SIEGE

Despite this bitterest of persecutions, within ten years the Anabaptist movement had reached the far corners of the German world. Entire regions of southern Germany, all of ancient Swabia, the Tyrol, Salzburg, Württemberg, Bavaria, Ansbach, and the Palatine Electorate, as well as central Germany including Hessen, Thuringia and Saxony had been affected. The movement spread along the Lower Rhine region into The Netherlands and 'Belgium' and along the Baltic Sea to East Prussia. Cities too were affected as the faith branched out quickly from Zürich to Strasbourg, Augsburg, Regensburg, Salzburg, and Worms. Soon afterwards, it reached Aachen, Gent, Utrecht, Amsterdam, Emden, Hamburg, Lübeck, Danzig, and even Königsberg (now Kaliningrad) in East Prussia.

As the authorities clamped down, followers were driven out of the cities and became nomads, forming small, closed communities. Their conviction was reinforced by key Anabaptist thinkers who developed the creed into a much wider religious philosophy.[5] Foremost amongst these thinkers was Melchior Hoffman, an itinerant furrier who took up residence in Strasbourg in 1530.

1.2. Melchior Hoffman. (Engraving by Christoffel van Sichem, before 1608. Courtesy of Rijksmuseum, Amsterdam)

At this time Strasbourg was one of the largest cities in the Holy Roman Empire and its city council appeared to have had a high tolerance for dissenters. Many Anabaptist refugees from other parts of Europe, particularly the Swiss Confederacy and southern German areas, began pouring into the city. Hoffman declared that he was one of the 'two witnesses' of the Book of Revelation, that the end of the world was nigh, and that Strasbourg was about to become the 'New Jerusalem', ruling the entire world. In addition to repudiating infant baptism, followers promised to redeem their worldly goods in collective trust and to give any surplus to the poor, to adopt a modest and simple dress and to embrace non-violence.

It was perhaps inevitable that the development of the Anabaptist creed would need to engage in some way with the political and social realities of the day and Hoffman found it difficult to maintain the pacifist leanings of most

---

5   For a discussion see Andrew Drummond, *The Dreadful History and Judgement of God on Thomas Müntzer* (London and New York: Verso, 2024).

'A MIGHTY FORTRESS OF GOD': THE SIEGE OF MÜNSTER 1534-35

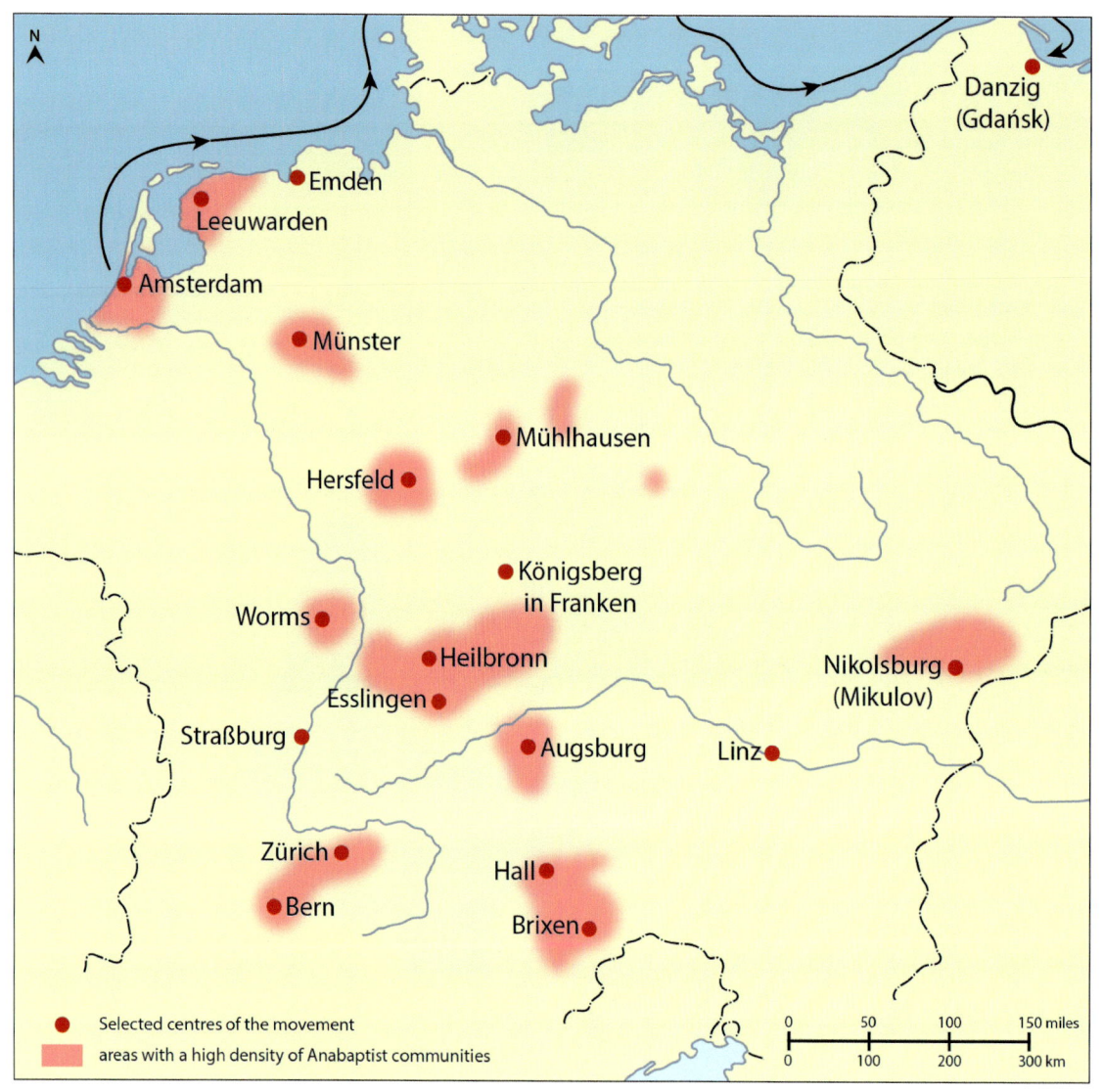

M.1.2. The Spread of Anabaptism. (Courtesy: Maximilian Dörrbecker)

THE RISE OF ANABAPTISM AND THE CAUSES OF THE SIEGE

Anabaptist groups, proclaiming the right of the elect to employ the sword against the worldly authorities, "the godless," and the "enemies of the saints".[6] This made Anabaptism particularly attractive to the downtrodden and, as he travelled throughout Germany preaching his gospel, Hoffman had a significant impact in the northwest and on into The Netherlands where it gained a foothold in Amsterdam, Leeuwarden, Antwerp and Groningen in Friesland in particular. He proclaimed the end of the year 1533 as the date that would see the second coming of Christ and the casting down of the mighty from their seats of wealth and privilege. This was very much part of an apocalyptic world view in which crisis, suffering and catastrophe were expected in a world polarized between the forces of ultimate good and ultimate evil. Apocalyptic believers were strengthened by a hope in God's imminent intervention and within this, *prophecy* became a particularly important element. Prophets were not confined to theologians or trained pastors but could emerge from the ranks of lay men and women,[7] and they could assume the role as intermediaries between God and the believers and thereby exert a great deal of influence.

Such was the anticipation amongst the poorer sections of the Strasbourg population that the authorities feared a popular uprising and had Hoffman imprisoned in one of the towers on the city wall. During his imprisonment from which he was never released, 'Melchiorite' missionaries were venturing forth from Strasbourg, amongst them a key organiser by the name of Jan Matthijs.

1.3. Jan Matthys was a baker from Haarlem, in The Holy Roman Empire's County of Holland, and was converted to Anabaptism through the ministry of Melchior Hoffman in the 1520s. Matthys baptised thousands of converts, and after Hoffman's imprisonment, rose to prominence, rejecting Hoffman's pacifism and non-violence arguing that oppression had to be met with resistance. He was to be brutally killed by the Bishop's landsknechts having led a deluded foray with a small troop of men beyond the city walls of Münster during the early stages of the siege. (Engraving by Christoffel van Sichem 1677. Courtesy: of the Rijksmuseum, Amsterdam)

---

6   Belfort Bax, cf. https://www.marxists.org/archive/bax/1903/anabaptists/ch04.htm (accessed 29 August 2023).

7   Willem de Bakker, Michael Driedger and James Stayer, *Bernhard Rothmann and the Reformation in Münster, 1530-35* (Kitchener: Pandora Press 2009), pp.43-46.

'A MIGHTY FORTRESS OF GOD': THE SIEGE OF MÜNSTER 1534-35

1.4. Münster, panorama by Georg Braun and Frans Hogenberg (engraved between 1572 and 1618). It shows the city from the southwest, with the main churches dominating the skyline. From left to right: Liebfrauenkirche, St Paul's Cathedral (in the centre), Lambertikirche, Ludgerikirche. (Public domain)

When it transpired at the end of 1533 that Strasbourg was after all not destined to be the New Jerusalem, attention switched to the city of Münster in Westphalia, where events were developing with astounding rapidity, and where the belief was growing among Anabaptists in this corner of the Holy Roman Empire that this city rather than Strasbourg was ordained to be the seat of the future 'Kingdom of God'. How did this come about?

At the beginning of the sixteenth century the Bishopric of Münster was an important ecclesiastical state with its government in the hands of the prince-bishop and of the chapter of the diocese based in the city cathedral. The members of the chapter were recruited solely from the local nobility (clerics and the knighthood) and it enjoyed a great degree of political autonomy within The Empire. However, in the cities the power and privilege of the clergy had begun to be challenged by a new interest group – the guilds – and their representation on the municipal council. The clergy's exemption from taxation and military service and its ability to compete commercially with the guilds was a source of ongoing tension in the city councils, none more so than in Münster. This had found expression during the Peasants' War of 1525–26 in a number of northern cities,[8] and in Münster the guilds had led an attack on a monastery which had entered commercial competition with them, forcing them to make very considerable concessions.

However, following the defeat of the peasant and urban artisan uprising in 1525, the northern bishoprics had been able to regain their lost power with any concessions made to the municipal guilds being

---

[8] The social structure and wellbeing of the peasantry had not given cause to the mass uprisings such as those that occurred in Central and Southern Germany and the Tyrol. Cf Werner Freitag, 'Warum gab es in Westfalen keinen Bauernkrieg?' in *Wochenblatt für Landwirtschaft und Landleben,* 12, (2018), p.106. https://www.wochenblatt.com/dl/2/3/3/0/6/2/7/2018-12-Wochenblatt_Reformation21.pdf (accessed 4 July 2023).

THE RISE OF ANABAPTISM AND THE CAUSES OF THE SIEGE

swiftly withdrawn. Then, in 1529, an outbreak of the 'Black Death' devastated Westphalia and crop failures led to a trebling of the price of rye. On top of this came the imposition of an extraordinary tax in 1530 to finance the military response to the Turkish invasion of the eastern territories of The Holy Roman Empire. There was once again cause for unrest and opposition to the authorities.

In 1531 a new priest by the name of Bernd Rothmann[9] came to Münster whose anti-clericalism and Lutheranism proved attractive to increasing numbers of his congregation. Finding support in the guilds and a patrician by the name of Bernd Knipperdolling, Rothmann was instrumental a year later in bringing about a council decision to appoint Lutheran preachers in the ten churches in the city, prompting the cathedral chapter to leave Münster. In August 1532, Bishop Franz von Waldeck began to take action against the city, confiscating goods owned by Münster merchants. This prompted the city council to hire mercenaries and commission work on Münster's fortifications. On 26 December 1532, there was an abortive attempt by a group of Münster burghers to kidnap the Bishop. By the turn of the year, it was becoming clear to von Waldeck that he was unable to make the populace abandon its new faith and on 14 February he reluctantly officially recognised the city as Lutheran – a state of affairs which was not to last long, however.

1.5. The City Hall of Münster, located in the centre of Prinzipalmarkt, became the focal point of the political and religious machinations leading to the siege. Photo dated c. 1900; The City Hall was destroyed during WW2. (Wikimedia Commons. CC BY-SA 4.0)

Rothmann's sermons and writings were becoming particularly attractive for the Melchiorites and Jan Matthijs[10] who, if anything, was more radical than Hoffman in his readiness to incite rebellion as a religious duty. Within a month of the arrest of Hoffman in June 1533, Matthijs, who was still in Amsterdam, had assumed leadership of the Dutch Anabaptists and with his sights set on Münster as the new Kingdom of God, sent four 'apostles' ahead of him to convert the ordinary folk and sound out the religious sympathies of the city's leaders. Language problems were eased by the widespread use of Plattdeutsch across the region. On 5 January 1534, they began to baptise the believers of Münster. The situation developed fast.

Amongst Matthijs' most intimate followers was a John (Jan) Bockelson, a tailor and erstwhile actor from Leiden. Scarcely 25 years old, he threw

---

9 Willem de Bakker, Michael Driedger and James Stayer, *Bernhard Rothmann and the Reformation in Münster, 1530-35* (Kitchener: Pandora Press 2009), pp.43-46.
10 cf Willem de Bakker, Michael Driedger and James Stayer, *Bernhard Rothmann and the Reformation in Münster, 1530-35* (Kitchener: Pandora Press 2009), pp.43-46.

'A MIGHTY FORTRESS OF GOD': THE SIEGE OF MÜNSTER 1534-35

1.6. Bernd Knipperdolling. (Engraving by Heinrich Aldegrever, 1536, courtesy of the Rijksmuseum, Amsterdam)

himself with ardour into the Anabaptist agitation, paying a short visit to the city in July 1533 but setting up domicile there on 13 January 1534. Within a short space of time, he had married Berndt Knipperdolling's daughter.

On 23 January Bishop von Waldeck demanded that the baptisers be arrested. However, following a confrontation between Anabaptists, Lutherans and Catholics, the council issued an accord on the mutual toleration of Anabaptists and Lutherans on 10 February. Sometime late in February, self-proclaimed prophet Jan Matthijs entered the city. The council elections on 23 February resulted in a pro-Anabaptist chamber with Berndt Knipperdolling elected as mayor. Four days later the council passed a law that all adults who refused baptism upon confession of faith had to leave the city. Some 2,000 Catholics and Lutherans went into exile. As news spread of the official toleration of Anabaptists in the city, hundreds, and soon thousands, of newly baptised believers began to come on foot, by boat, and on horseback from all over the Low Countries in search of this safe haven.

The *de facto* toleration by the city council of adult baptism meant that intervention by the Bishop and the Emperor Karl V (Charles V) would be inevitable. This was a flagrant breach of the Imperial Decree and for the Bishop, unless action was taken, any intervention by the Emperor would likely lead to the eventual incorporation of the diocese into the Burgundian territories, something he wished to avoid. Franz von Waldeck was compelled to act, lest the cathedral chapter report his indecisiveness to the Emperor. Following an unsuccessful attempt to take the city by surprise on 10 February,[11] the Bishop decided at some point between 14 and 17 February to announce his intention to lay siege to the city.

---

11 *Heinrich Gresbeck* (Christopher S. Mackay trans. and added commentary), *False Prophets and Preachers: Henry Gresbeck's Account of the Anabaptist Kingdom of Münster* (Kirksville: Truman State University Press, 2016), pp.64–65.

2

A Mighty Fortress – The Fortification of Münster

Located in what today is the northern part of the German state of North Rhine-Westphalia, Münster's historical location at a crossroads and ford on the River Aa had enabled it to become an important commercial centre. However it was the establishment of a cathedral in 857, enhanced by a library and a school, which gave it prominence as a religious centre in the region. It stood in a close relationship with several nearby ecclesiastical principalities notably Cologne, Paderborn, Osnabrück, Hildesheim, and Liège. Two fires in 1097 and 1121 had destroyed the entire settlement however, and when the bishop granted the city its town charter around 1173/1178, he decided to surround the entire settlement with a wall to serve both as a defensive structure and symbol of his power. By 1200 it had become a wealthy Hanseatic citadel with a City wall eight to ten metres high and over four kilometres long, enhanced with a moat, 10 gates, and 6 towers and enclosing an area of 102 hectares including the settlement areas on the left bank of the River Aa.

The city had originally displayed the classic medieval form of fortification – concentric circuits of walls punctuated by towers and gatehouses and surrounded either by a ditch or a moat. Between 1320 and 1340 a 4km long outer rampart with an outer ditch had been constructed with semi-circular bulwarks as a reinforcement against firearms which were at the time in their infancy. This so-called *fausse braye* consisted of a low outer wall of masonry, timber or sods, packed up behind with rammed earth, which served to defend the outer moat.

As siege weaponry developed into artillery with enhanced firepower, it became increasingly necessary to improve the city's fortifications.[1] During the fifteenth century the bulwarks in front of the gates had been reinforced

---

1   Christopher Duffy, *Siege Warfare*, (London: Routledge Kegan Paul 1979), p.2. Also see Appendix 5.

'A MIGHTY FORTRESS OF GOD': THE SIEGE OF MÜNSTER 1534-35

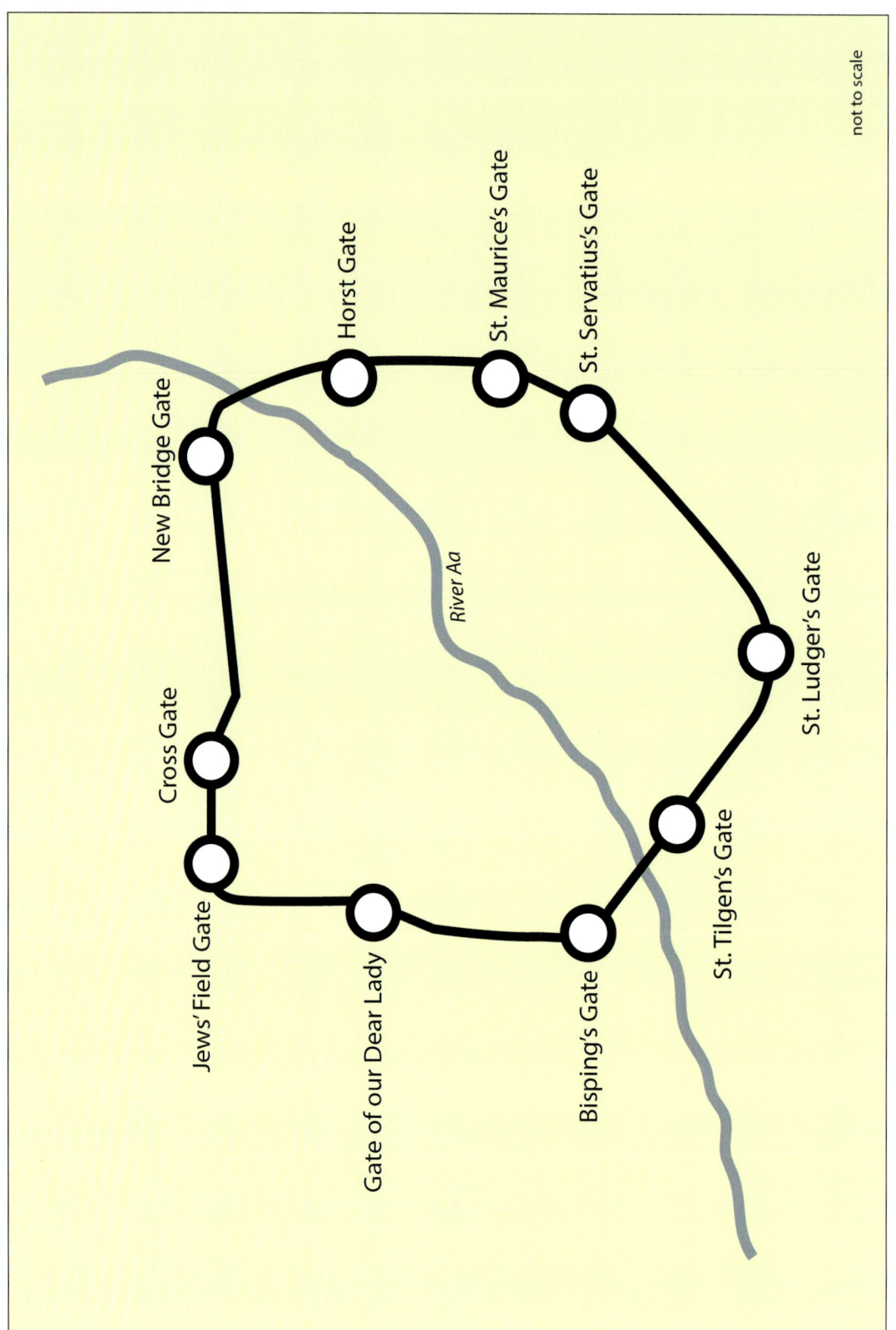

M.2. The Gatehouses of Münster

A MIGHTY FORTRESS – THE FORTIFICATION OF MÜNSTER

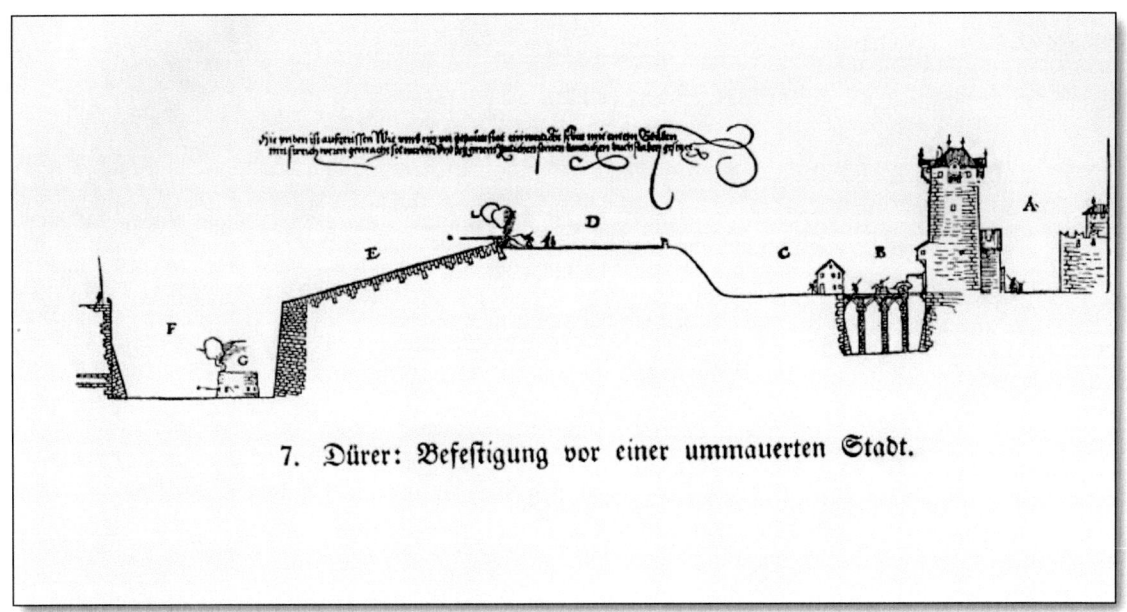

2.1. Cross section of a design for outer fortification from Albrecht Dürer's *Befestigungslehre* 1527.[2] Early modern European fortresses were so constructed as to keep any potential assailant under the fire of the defenders until the last possible moment. On level ground, troops attacking any high fortification enjoyed a higher degree of shelter from fire the nearer they were to the base of the wall. Outer defences were therefore constructed with a *glacis* – a slope with a low grade inclined towards the top of the wall. This gave defenders a direct line of sight onto the assaulting force, allowing them to efficiently sweep the field with fire from the parapet. Moreover, an angled embankment would weaken the impact of artillery fire. The side of the outer defence facing the curtain wall had a lower battlement to enable damage to any attacking force which had overwhelmed it. Free standing roundels and *ravelins* would have a ramp and or stairs on the curtain wall side to facilitate the movement of troops and artillery into position on this outer fortification.

as city fortifications underwent a period of transition, with military engineers being tasked with reducing the vulnerability of the classic late medieval walled city. It had become clear that the wall towers were too high, outer walls too thin, and whereas cities increasingly used handguns, burning pitch and other projectiles to repulse their attackers, these were now proving useless against siege guns with sufficient calibre to pound a city from a safe distance. Logically the time had arrived for defenders to make use of the same weaponry, but existing battlements in many walled cities, Münster included, were generally too weak and too devoid of the necessary space and structural integrity to accommodate the new artillery. Thus, the city defences required some reconfiguration. At the beginning of 1520 work had commenced on the construction of the great bulwark (*Zwinger*) at the exit of the River Aa and a decade later the bastion known as the *Neuwerk* was erected in front of the Bisping Gate.

---

2   Dürer Albrecht, *Etliche Unterricht zur Befestigung der Stadt, Schloss und Flecken* (Nördlingen: Verlag Dr Alfons Uhl, 1980)

'A MIGHTY FORTRESS OF GOD': THE SIEGE OF MÜNSTER 1534-35

2.2. Albrecht Dürer's design for a Bastion from *Befestigungslehre 1527*. As the need to 'fight fire with fire' soon became apparent, the old fortifications had another serious disadvantage. The installation of artillery on the battlements of the city walls was going to require the construction of wider and sturdier fortifications. The solution therefore had to be the creation of separate locations on the walls which offered sufficient space and stability to provide cannon with the necessary range of fire and effect. This objective became the central theme of fortification construction, leading initially to the development of the so-called roundel. As the name suggests, this was a semi-circular bastion, in some cases achieved by thickening the masonry of existing towers. These bastions flared outwards, again in the interests of presenting an inclined surface, and the crenelations along the top were replaced by curved or bevelled parapets. They could have several floors. Dürer is known to have travelled to Italy in 1494 and 1505, but failed to venture as far as Florence or Rome where the most advanced developments in fortification were to be found. Hence his military architecture remains an isolated North European attempt to meet the challenge of problems that were already finding more convincing solutions in Italy.

The medieval angular towers were slowly abandoned in favour of cylindrical constructions, which offered a glancing surface to cannon shot. Where complete rebuilding of the curtain walls was undertaken, these too would be inclined, thickened, and provided with embrasures and vaulted casemates for cannon. The inner curtain wall would be connected to any outer fortifications by structures known as *caponiers*. These were covered passageways equipped with ports for handguns and cannon ports to permit fire along the intervening ditch. Since the *fausse braye* could be easier to climb, the ditch or moat was widened to expose any attacking infantry to fire from a higher elevation, including enfilading fire from the bastions. It was not uncommon for smaller freestanding advanced defence works such as *tenailles* or sconces[3] to pepper the approach to a city's fortifications.

---

3 French for the tip of a pair of pincers. Sconces were the early modern era's equivalent of pillboxes.

A MIGHTY FORTRESS – THE FORTIFICATION OF MÜNSTER

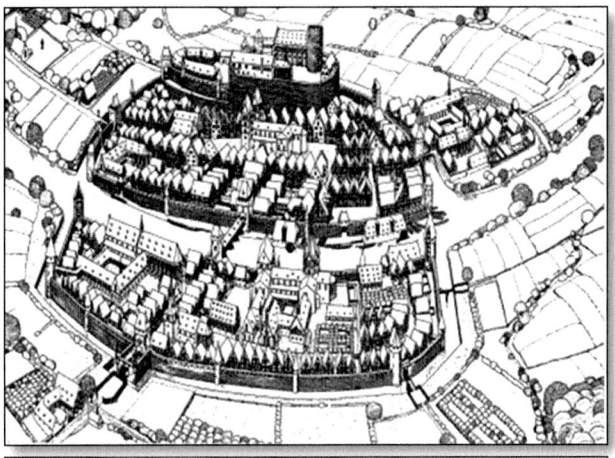
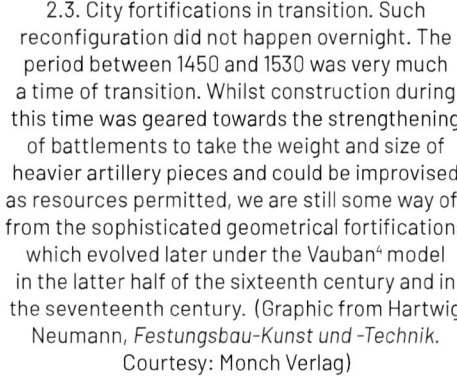

2.3. City fortifications in transition. Such reconfiguration did not happen overnight. The period between 1450 and 1530 was very much a time of transition. Whilst construction during this time was geared towards the strengthening of battlements to take the weight and size of heavier artillery pieces and could be improvised as resources permitted, we are still some way off from the sophisticated geometrical fortifications which evolved later under the Vauban[4] model in the latter half of the sixteenth century and in the seventeenth century. (Graphic from Hartwig Neumann, *Festungsbau-Kunst und -Technik*. Courtesy: Monch Verlag)

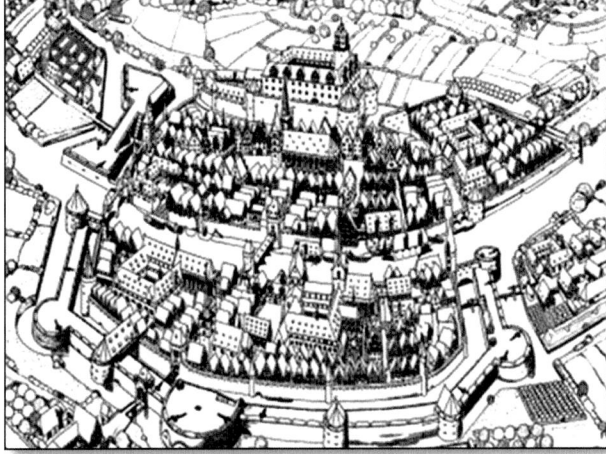

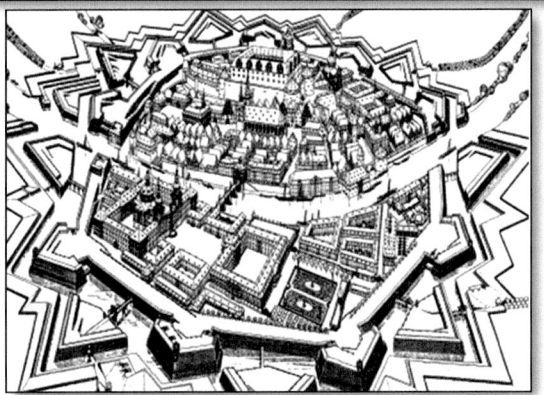

These were built of many materials, usually earth and brick, to withstand the impact of a cannonball.

---

4   Sébastien Le Prestre de Vauban commonly referred to as Vauban, was a French military engineer and *Maréchal de France* who worked under Louis XIV. He is generally considered the greatest engineer of his time. Cf William Allingham, *The New Method of Fortification, as Practised by Monsieur de Vauban Engineer-*

'A MIGHTY FORTRESS OF GOD': THE SIEGE OF MÜNSTER 1534-35

2.4. Woodcut by Erhard Schön 1535 showing the bastions and outer defences at Münster. (LWL-Museum für Kunst und Kultur, Westfälisches Landesmuseum, Münster)

In general, towers began to be reduced in height, and additionally the walls were thickened – particularly on the middle floor of a tower, where the line of fire was almost straight and provided the most optimal impact for a siege cannon with a calibre which enabled it to be positioned at a safe distance from the city walls.

Whilst the semi-circular bastions presented a formidable defence, they nevertheless brought with them limitations in a close-range assault where the besieger could freely plant his ladders and begin mining in the dead ground at the salient of the adjacent roundel. This dead angle had to be eliminated, so that a constant stream of fire could be maintained covering every angle of an assault. Hence this form eventually was to give way to a triangular shaped earthwork specifically designed to cover the adjacent counterpart (See Plate 1). They were styled very much on the Italian approach to defensive construction known as the *Trace Italienne* which appear in the fortifications of the Italian town of Sarzanello, and dates from 1497.[5] This system enabled lines of fire from all angles on the walls and such bastions were often detached and located in front of the inner works of a fortress.

General of France. Together with a New Treatise of Geometry, (Farmington Hills, Gale ECCO, 2018).

5   NB Also mirrored by the Dutch military engineers.

A MIGHTY FORTRESS – THE FORTIFICATION OF MÜNSTER

The *Trace Italienne* was very much the forerunner of the Vauban system of fortification preferred by an increasing number of European cities in the sixteenth and seventeenth centuries.

In Germany, *ravelins*, the triangular structures which characterised the *Trace Italienne*, were known as *Brückenköpfe* or bridgeheads where they were built as small forts supposed to protect the bridge that led across the moat to the city or fortress gate from a direct attack. However, it was not until the German fortress builder Daniel Specklin (1536–1589) recognized the principal importance of *ravelins* that they were made as large as possible so that they fully covered the curtain wall of the city to provide flanking fire

2.5. The *Zwinger* in Münster. The only remaining bastion in the city which dates to the siege. *Zwingers* were originally outer courtyard areas between two defensive walls that were used as 'kill zones'. The word derives from *zwingen* meaning 'to force', and certainly such bastions on the outer works forced an enemy to negotiate it before they could assault the main defensive line. (Photo: Author)

2.6. Examples of outer defences.
Various modes of outer defences as illustrated by Ludwig Eyb vom Hartenstein – a mix of these would have been used on the palisade on top of the outer wall. (*Kriegs- u. Feuerwerkbuch* 1500; Ms H2/MS.B 26. Courtesy, University Library Erlangen)

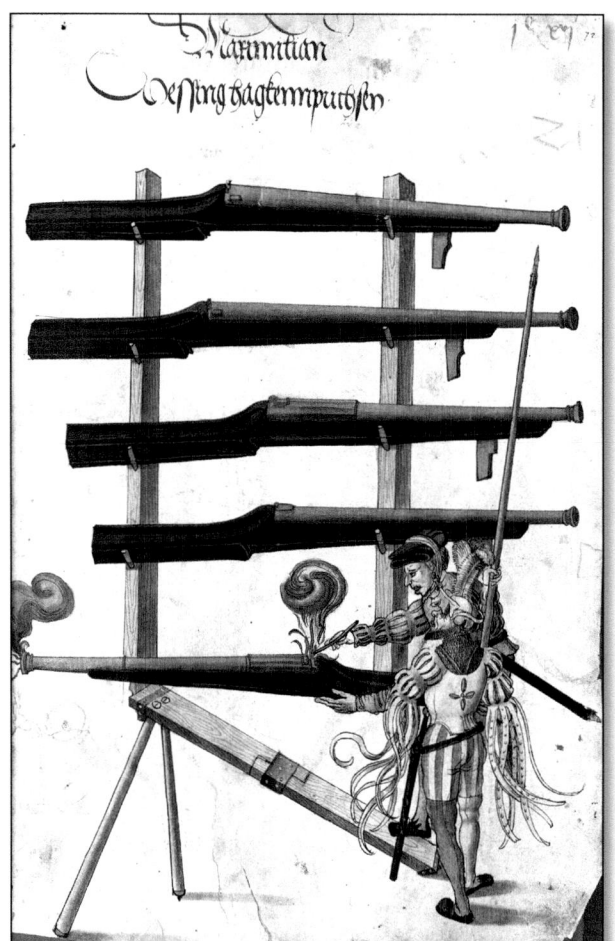

2.7. Wall Guns – a rack containing a number of larger calibre hand guns also known as hook guns (*Doppelhaken*) because of the lug or hook at the end of the barrel for steadying the weapon on a parapet or palisade. (*Zeugbuch Kaiser Maximilians BSB Cod.icon 222*. Courtesy, Bayerische Staatsbibliothek).

in front of the bastions. The pointed nature of the *ravelin* served to split up an assault force and enable city artillery to fire upon the attacking troops as they approached the curtain wall. However, it must be noted that the outer works of the city's defences at the time of the Anabaptist commune would not have been configured in this way.

Most representations of the fortification of the city have been based on Evert Alerdinck's highly detailed etching created in 1636 (see plate one). By this time Münster had embraced the Vauban system of *ravelins* with outer works with solid embrasures. At the time of the siege, however, the outer defences would have looked somewhat different as Kerssenbroch describes below:

> The whole city is surrounded by twin ditches, which are fairly broad and deep. While the first ditch abuts onto the open fields and gardens, the second one, which is dug out on the other side of a rampart, is equipped in various locations with assorted barriers,

barricades, defensive works, and swallows' cages,[6] so that it would allow no enemy, however violent, to pass. In between the two ditches there is a rampart made of earth dug up from both ditches. This rampart is thick and steep and has a sheer face. It encloses the second (inner) ditch with a continuous circuit and is crowned on its ridge and high point with a wooden stockade that has teeth on top. A little bit lower down, not very far from the water, a thicket of dense, bristling briers and intertwined brambles goes around, and not only can this not be penetrated but it is not even possible to see through it. These two defences will easily check the ascent of those who have already crossed the ditch. The rampart also has within it very many shelters, hidden passageways, and concealed tunnels from which the enemy can be attacked on all sides with guns and pikes.... Next, there is a double wall whose circuit is broken only at the gates. These walls surround another rampart, which is set between and supported by them on either side. One wall is close to the second ditch.[7]

Münster's fortifications were thus going to present a major challenge to the Bishop in terms of laying a siege. His priority in the early weeks following his announcement was to assemble a siege army and mount a blockade to control the traffic entering and leaving Münster's gates.

---

6   Described as a type of blockhouse 'made of strong timber and resting on beams, being full of loopholes on both sides'. p.100.
7   Hermann von Kerssenbroch, (Christopher S. Mackay tr.), *Narratio Historica Anabaptistici Furoris Monasterium*, (*Narrative of the Anabaptist Madness. The overthrow of Münster, the Famous Metropolis of Westphalia*) (Leiden–Boston: Brill, 2007), p.102.

3

The Bishop's Siege preparations

Bishop Franz von Waldeck had begun initial recruitment for action against the city as early as winter 1532/33, commissioning four companies under the command of William of Arnhem, Egbert of Deveren, Evert Ovelacker and Dirick von Zwolle. Reports back to Philipp of Hessen reckoned this force to number 1500 men.[1] On 17 February, the Bishop issued a secret order to his nobility to be 'prepared in the strongest possible terms' to defend the diocese. He estimated, somewhat naively, a period of service of one to two months. On 18 February he authorised his first recruiting officers.

Recruitment

Whilst rumours of this mobilisation began circulating in Münster and had a galvanising effect on the various political factions within the city, Bishop von Waldeck summoned his nobility to his new headquarters in Telgte, to the east of the city. Here he appointed Johann von Bueren, Herman von Mengerssen, Gerd Morrien and Johann von Raesfield as members of his council of war. Only 30 knights answered the Bishop's initial call – pitching camp on 27 February at Evekinghof Manor (Haus Nevinghof) north of the city from where they commenced guard duty. On 28 February, the Bishop once again appealed to the entire knighthood within his diocese and 26 nobles presented themselves for immediate duty at Telgte. A further 54 were to take up position at Nienberge. The remaining 59 nobles were ordered to assemble at Wolbeck on 2 March. Bishop von Waldeck was eager to establish strategically placed encampments for both his mercenaries and his light horse. The encampments are shown in Map 3.

---

1 Karl-Heinz Kirchhoff, 'Die Belagerung und Eroberung Münsters 1534/35' in *Westfälische Zeitschrift* volume 112 (1962) p.78.

THE BISHOP'S SIEGE PREPARATIONS

The Bishop ordered roadblocks to be set up on the approaches to the city to prevent the Anabaptists from recruiting landsknechts and to block the import of any foodstuffs. The city responded promptly with an attack on 25 February launched from the St Maurice gate onto a newly set up landsknecht camp that was seen as a key base for the besiegers. The attack destroyed the camp – temporarily.

The nobility felt obliged to respond to this second urgent call up from the Bishop and reported for duty during the first week of March. Bernd von Westerholt, Dirick von der Recke and Hermann von Bilrebeck were given command of the Bishop's horse. Twenty horsemen reinforced the contingent at Nevinghof while Westerholt and Recke billeted with 45 men at the manors of Kaldenhof and Lütkenbeck. Bilrebeck camped with some 222 mounted troops at the village of Roxel. Altogether 169 nobles had responded to the bishop's call. Each of them would have been accompanied by two or three bodyguards and between two and eight, mounted, vassals.[2]

When the first muster was conducted at the Hohe Schemme on 27 March, 34 knights, 85 foot and 145 light horse were listed as being quartered in the Roxel camp. 70 were based at the manor of Kaldenhof, supported by 269 horse and 172 foot. The monthly pay per man and horse was eight Emden guilders.[3] On 18 February, Wilken Steding was appointed supreme commander of the Bishop's army and, supported with

3.1. Bishop Franz von Waldeck (1492–1553). A descendant of the Counts of Waldeck, he studied at the University of Erfurt (1506) becoming canon in Trier, Cologne, Mainz and Paderborn, provost of Einbeck (1521), administrator of Minden (1530), before his election as Bishop of Münster (and Osnabrück) on 1 June 1532, vowing to act against the Reformation movement. In 1533 he came to an accommodation with the Münster Protestants, but the election of an Anabaptist council was a step too far prompting him to lay siege to the city. The Bishop, with the Prince-Bishoprics of Münster, Osnabrück and Minden, held in his hands the largest mass of lands in the northwest of The Empire, second only to the Herzog von Jülich-Kleve-Berg. (Oil on canvass, c. 1660. Schloss Iburg © Staatliches Baumanagement Region Nord-West)

---

2 Karl-Heinz Kirchhoff, 'Die Belagerung und Eroberung Münsters 1534/35' in *Westfälische Zeitschrift* volume 112 (1962) p.78.
3 Originally the gold guilder of the East Frisian city of Emden. Towards the middle of the sixteenth century, the Emden guilder developed into a coin of account.

'A MIGHTY FORTRESS OF GOD': THE SIEGE OF MÜNSTER 1534-35

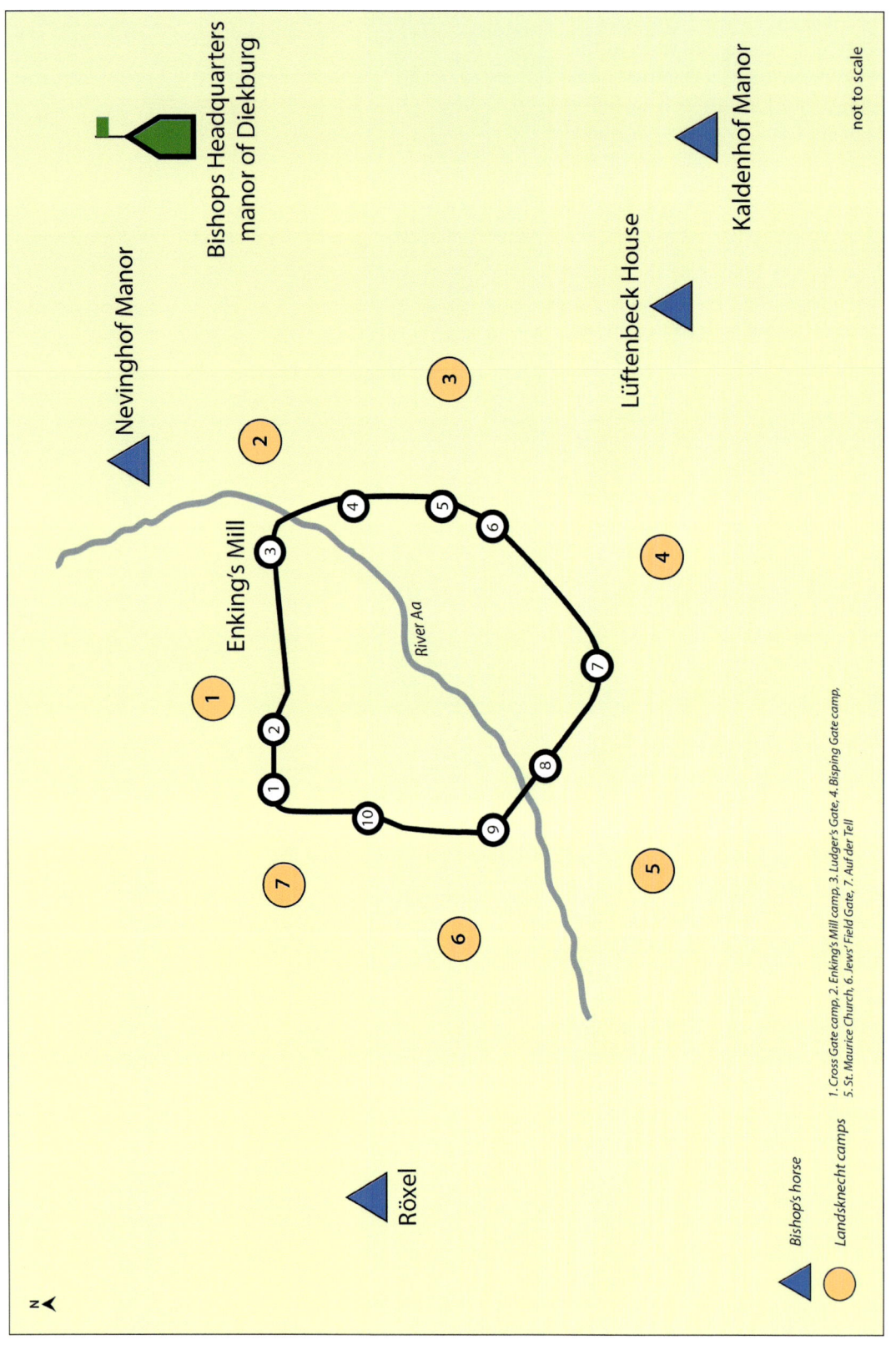

M.3. The Bishop's initial camps, based on Kirchhoff's sketches.

1. Cross Gate camp, 2. Enking's Mill camp, 3. Ludger's Gate, 4. Bisping Gate camp, 5. St. Maurice Church, 6. Jews' Field Gate, 7. Auf der Tell

THE BISHOP'S SIEGE PREPARATIONS

3.2. Light horsemen, woodcut by Erhard Schön. (Public domain)

funds from Philipp, Landgraf von Hessen, set about recruiting mercenaries from as far afield as Meissen and Thuringia. On 13 March, around 150 men arrived for duty before the gates of Münster. Three more companies of mercenaries were raised with the support of Elector Johann Friedrich of Saxony and they mustered in Kreuzberg in late March. Captain and magistrate Johann Dankelmann began recruiting in the Rhineland and returned with further contingents in mid-March. The Captains Pilgrim von Iselmude and Gerhard von Münster undertook wider recruitment activity in The Netherlands. News of the Bishop's declaration of war had spread

'A MIGHTY FORTRESS OF GOD': THE SIEGE OF MÜNSTER 1534-35

3.3. Landsknecht pikemen and handgunners, woodcut by Erhard Schön. (Public domain)

and by the end of February groups of unattached *freie landsknechte* were beginning to appear in the area.[4]

The Bishop's officials were under strict instructions to ensure that these landsknechts were recruited for his service, lest they defect to the Anabaptists.

> In spite of our various writs of command, we find that through your and other of our officials' neglect, foreign help and servants are secretly and obviously coming to Münster almost every day …. and [I] therefore want to remind you once again of your oaths and obligations to the highest degree and order you, with the help of your official commanders and territorial people, not to allow any foreign people or servants to pass through, except those who come to us for the best and have a passport or writing. For if you are found to be in default after these days and this strengthens those of Münster, we will repay you with severe punishment and disgrace.[5]

---

4 Karl-Heinz Kirchhoff, 'Die Belagerung und Eroberung Münsters 1534/35' in *Westfälische Zeitschrift* volume 112 (1962) p.80.

5 Order dated 8 March from the Bishop to his commanders. cf Richard van Dülmen, *Das Täuferreich zu Münster 1534-1535: Berichte und Dokumente* (Munich Deutscher Taschenbuch Verlag, 1974) p.89.

THE BISHOP'S SIEGE PREPARATIONS

Bishop von Waldeck made a special effort to enlist those officers who had previously served for him, but they were currently in East Friesland in the pay of King Christian III of Denmark and the Graf von Friesland, or were serving on the opposite side under the Herzog von Guelders. On 23 March, the dispute between Guelders and East Friesland was temporarily settled at Alfeld, and the Bishop was swift in recruiting the Captains Walter von Deventer, Lenz von der Horst, Arnd von Utrecht, von Kyll and Claes Utermark and their men into his service. Egbert von Deveren, Oswald Münster, Bernd Kettel and Dirick van Tyll with their Guelders contingents also joined. At the end of April, the companies recruited by Wilken Steding in Saxony under Albrecht Pelzke (aka Beltz), Jorien, and Lyppelt von Wolframstorp and Michael von Erfort assembled before Münster. They were finally joined in mid-May by a company of 600 men under Evert Ovelacker and in June by an auxiliary force of 1,000 men from Cleves under Captain Hermann von Sittard. Each company of 200 mercenaries had 20 auxiliaries referred to as 'men of lower rank'. The basic salary was four guilders, so a company cost approximately 1,000 guilders per month. By the summer of 1535, the total number of mercenaries in the army stood at between 7,000 and 8,000 and cost 34,000 Emden guilders per month in pay.[6]

Siegeworks in the Early Modern Era

The changes occurring in the fortification of cities in the early modern era called for new ways of organising a siege. When a besieging army arrived at its objective, squadrons of horse would be sent to surround the city and set up roadblocks at all roads leading in. As was common in military engagements of the period, there would be an initial attempt at parley, although demands to surrender were rarely heeded. Rejection by the defenders generally meant the construction of lines of earthworks. This task usually fell to teams of sappers often recruited from farm workers and, occasionally, miners. Early in the siege of Münster Saxon miners were recruited at landsknecht pay to undertake the digging work.

Normally a siege army would construct earthwork lines at 2,400 metres from the defences with one line facing inward to guard against sorties from the defending city garrison (so-called *lines of circumvallation*) and one line facing outward to protect the besiegers from any enemy forces that might be attempting to break the siege from the outside (*lines of contravallation*). It would be some months before such work could be completed around Münster.

---

6   The detail on captains and their contingents could be taken from the accounts administered by Johannes Hageboke the Bishop's *Pfennigmeister*. cf Ernst Müller (ed.), 'Die Abrechnung des Johannes Hageboke über die Kosten der Belagerung der Stadt Münster 1534-1535 …' in *Veröffentlichungen der Historischen Kommission des Provinzialinstituts für Westfälische Landes- und Volkskunde III,* (Münster: Aschendorffsche Verlagsbuchhandlung, 1937).

'A MIGHTY FORTRESS OF GOD': THE SIEGE OF MÜNSTER 1534-35

The swearing-in took place in the Bishop's presence and by which the mercenaries agreed to abide by 30 rules of engagement (see Appendix I). Although most mercenaries brought their own weapons with them, the Bishop had ordered the delivery of 2,422 pikes, 124 double length arquebuses (*Doppelhaken*) and 535 smaller matchlocks, as well as large quantities of powder, lead shot, and other munitions.

Command Structure

Members of the Council of War (including Commanders of foot and horse.)
Ritter Johann van Bueren
Freiherr Gerhard von Morrien
Hermann von Mengersheim
Dicarius of the Bishopric of Paderborn
Johann von Raesfeld

Commanders of the Horse
Johann von Rorthe
Johann von Senden
Johann von Dincklage

Commanders of the infantry
Wilhelm von Steding
Gerhard Schmocker (who defected to the rebels)

Company captains
Johann Corpner, Georg Schimmel, Johann Hake, Gottfried von Utrecht, Bernhard Rettel, George Ailen, Nicholaus Utermark, Jodolous Muth, Georg Wolframsstorf, Michael Effurth, Lippold Wolframsstorf, Reimanus Peregrinus, Andreas Lubbeke, Egbert Deveren, Theodorich Groll, Eberhard Overlacker, Hermann Sittard, Lorenz Horst, Theodor Eilen, Albert von Beltz, Augustin von Deventer.

Pay
4 Emden guilders for foot   8 for common horse / ensign 16[7]
One month was calculated as 28 days

---

[7]   Only the ensign is listed in the pay rates in the original source.

THE BISHOP'S SIEGE PREPARATIONS

3.4. Siege camps could appear quite haphazard as this woodcut of the Siege of Wolfenbüttel by Lucas Cranach the Younger shows. (Public domain)

Generally, supplies for a siege would be stored in fortified camps positioned strategically between the lines of earthworks. These were temporary structures made of a simple bank of earth fronted by a ditch and flanked by sconces. At the outset, the Bishop established three infantry camps:

- The first was located close to the ruins of St Mauritz church and placed under the command of Wilken Steding.
- The second was situated on the banks of the River Aa on the approach to the St Tilgen city gates. This was reinforced with troops from Meissen under the command of Albert Beltz.
- The third camp consisting of the Guelders contingents under the command of Egbert von Deveren and was established at the approach to the Judenfeld (Jews' Field) Gate.

In April and May, the blockade ring around Münster was completed with the erection of four other camps:

- Captain Johann Corritzer's contingent was positioned in front of the St Ludger Gate.
- Lorenz von der Horst's men were stationed front of the Cross gate.
- Evert Ovelacker's men were encamped at Enking's Mill.
- The final blockading camp under the command of Hermann Sittard occupied a dilapidated manor on the approach road to the Gate of Our Lady.

Beyond these seven camps a second 'ring' was set up consisting of the five bases for the Bishop's knights and light horse in the manors of Evekinghof (Nevinghof), Kaldenhof, Lütkenbeck and in the village of Roxel. In the space between, Johann de Korte was tasked with patrolling the roads with squadrons of light horse. The Bishop's Palace was in Telgte but the councils of war were held at the manor of Dyckburg, to the north-east of the city.

On 28 February, armed peasants were summoned from the nearby towns to bring shovels, axes and hooks in carts and ordered to speedily dig the initial earthworks for the camps. The parishes of the dioceses were ordered to supply 3,100 'good, strong, well-constructed wicker panels', along with 330 wheelbarrows and 2,200 shovels. A renewed call was made on 11 April to the peasants of nine parishes to assist with the construction of the siegeworks but only the Bocholt peasants came. The Bishop was forced to remind his subjects that unless they appeared they would face physical punishments. He instructed his bailiffs to carry out his orders and commanded his nobility to release their own subjects, and drillmasters were assigned to teach them the rudiments of military service. After the

THE BISHOP'S SIEGE PREPARATIONS

customary camp watches were set up, additional soldiers arrived at midnight and took up their positions.[8]

Wicker hurdles eight feet broad and twelve long were woven, and with beams placed underneath them, they were to be set up in various locations along the Aa, which flowed among the camps. Baskets (gabions) were also woven, and these would serve as obstructions against gunfire. For the coming assault the commanders procured a large number of carts, shovels, grappling hooks, and ladders fitted with hooks. The peasants were also summoned in gangs to dig entrenchments for the camps in relays. Some of them were ordered to bring loads of wicker and broom shrubs in worn-out wagons that they would leave in the camps, while others were ordered to bring stronger wagons laden with bundles of wood and bush, which they would take back home with them after unloading these wagons.[9]

3.5. Enking's Mill, modern day. (Photo: Frank Vincenz via Wikimedia Commons)

Meanwhile, to maintain discipline in the camps, the Prince-Bishop issued a command on 3 May to all the bailiffs and stewards throughout the diocese, ordering that those who left their companies without permission from their commanders and/or were attempting to decamp were to be seized en route as deserters and kept under arrest awaiting punishment. The bailiffs and stewards were also to keep an eye on the roads in all directions, to ensure that only enlisted soldiers among the Prince's contingents should be allowed to travel to the camps without

---

8   Hermann von Kerssenbroch (Christopher S. Mackay tr.), *Narratio Historica Anabaptistici Furoris Monasterium, Narrative of the Anabaptist Madness. The overthrow of Münster, the Famous Metropolis of Westphalia*. (Leiden–Boston: Brill 2007), p.546.
9   Hermann von Kerssenbroch (Christopher S. Mackay tr.), *Narratio Historica Anabaptistici Furoris Monasterium, Narrative of the Anabaptist Madness. The overthrow of Münster, the Famous Metropolis of Westphalia* (Leiden–Boston: Brill 2007), p.556.

3.6. Traders and Officers in a landsknecht camp from Mathias Gerung's oil painting of 1551, Feldlager Karls V. vor Lauingen 1546. (Photo: Hermann Müller. Courtesy: Heimathaus, Stadt Lauingen)

official permission. Those parishes which were some distance from the city were given special dispensation but were required to pay compensation in return. At the Nevinghof camp a free market was set up, to allow merchants from near and far to sell provisions to the landsknechts.

The cities of Osnabrück, Bielefeld, Lippstadt, Hamm, Dortmund, Unna, Geseke and Soest, the monastery of Paderborn and the Duchy of Westphalia were all asked to supply the camps. In addition, the parishes of Dülmen, Ahaus, Bevergern and Sassenberg were requisitioned to supply the Nevinghof camp, while the parishes of Wolbeck, Stromberg and Werne supplied the Kaldenhof camp. The parish of Horstmar was tasked with supplying the three infantry camps of St Mauritz, at the Jews' Field gate and St Tilgen's (aka Aegidii) gate. The main camp in Wolbeck received twenty fat oxen every week from the parishes. The merchants in the diocese were able to compensate through their trade in the camps for their lack of business with the city of Münster.

THE BISHOP'S SIEGE PREPARATIONS

3.7. The artillery positioned behind earthworks at Münster. Woodcut by Erhard Schön 1535. (LWL-Museum für Kunst und Kultur, Westfälisches Landesmuseum, Münster)

Siege Artillery

Because the Bishop possessed no artillery park of his own, he had to rely on assistance from various other quarters for heavy siege guns. In March, a heavy field piece (*Kartaune*) arrived from the fortified residence of the Prince Bishop at Ahaus, followed by two cannons from Coesfeld, two from Borken, and one from Bocholt. At Iburg castle a heavy cannon with the nickname *Vlegengeist* was especially cast. Two more heavy field guns were delivered from the Landgrave Philipp of Hessen and the Herzog von Cleves sent eight pieces of artillery. Count Arnd of Bentheim provided a demi-culverin and two field guns while the Archbishop of Cologne supplied four culverins and 'a field piece'. Count Simon of Lippe made a cannon and a mortar available. A further culverin was supplied by the city of Bielefeld and the municipalities of Deventer, Campen and Zwolle offered a total of six cannon and six culverins. In total the bishop had 42 pieces of artillery for the siege although the Bocholt culverin later exploded on firing. Gun emplacements were positioned at various points between the seven infantry camps – most notably before the Jews' Field, Hörster and the St Maurice gates.

Procurement of Munitions and Other Material

The bishop also sent men to towns and trading places to procure and purchase military supplies. Johann Hessenbroeck bought 122 barrels of gunpowder in Brabant; Johann Heerde brought 150 barrels from Amsterdam, Hermarm Tegeder 40 barrels and Melchior Bodegen 36 barrels. Others were sent to Cologne, Trier, Frankfurt, Neuss, Kaiserswerth to buy powder. Friedrich Vetter brought 189 hundredweight of saltpetre from Erfurt, and others brought a large quantity of saltpetre and sulphur from various cities. Some mills and workshops were specifically set up to manufacture gunpowder such as at Iburg and Osnabrück. Konrad Prange, judge at Arnsberg, and Johann Swerthen had several thousand hundredweight of iron cast into balls in the ironworks of the Bergland.[10]

Egbert Kaerbuck oversaw the production of stone cannon shot from local quarries. The Archbishop of Cologne, the Herzog von Cleves, the Landgraf von Hessen, the Count of Bentheim, the city of Osnabrück and other neighbouring cities sent master gunners. Officers were dispatched to procure thousands of iron nails, several hundred hundredweight of iron and lead, and an innumerate quantity of hand grenades, firearms, falconets plus some mortars. Several thousand pikes and of all kinds of rope, straw, hay, oats for horse feed, the finest nettle cloth for pennants, and leather for hoses and sacks for powder transport were also procured. A number of blacksmiths and carpenters were taken into service with cash payments.[11] The town of Coesfeld supplied beer and bread to the camps. As the siege wore on and there were delays in paying the Bishop's troops, a number of farms in the locality became prone to looting, and some 22 suppliers sought letters of protection from the Bishop.

In the early phase of the siege the Bishop's mercenaries began to suffer hardship in the camps because little of what was needed was being brought in. Foreign merchants and local farmers feared too much for their personal safety and their property, deeming the Bishop's troops to be nothing more than a band of brigands. When the Bishop was made aware of this, he had gallows, wheels and other tools of punishment erected at each camp as deterrents, and ordered the soldiers to abstain from all injustice, sacrilege, and robbery, so that the merchants could sell without fear and danger at a reasonable price for both parties. At the same time, in a letter dated 15 March, he promised traders everywhere safe passage to come and supply his camps with provisions.[12]

---

10 Ernst Müller(ed.), 'Die Abrechnung des Johannes Hageboke über die Kosten der Belagerung der Stadt Münster 1534-1535…' in *Veröffentlichungen der Historischen Kommission des Provinzialinstituts für westfälische Landes- und Volkskunde III*, (Münster: Aschendorffsche Verlagsbuchhandlung, 1937), p X.

11 Reinhard Baumann, *Landsknechte* (Munich: C.H. Beck Verlag. 1994), p.121.

12 Karl-Heinz Kirchhoff, 'Die Belagerung und Eroberung Münsters 1534/35' in *Westfälische Zeitschrift* volume 112 (1962), p.31.

THE BISHOP'S SIEGE PREPARATIONS

3.8. Coloured Woodcut of two master gunners, plate 133r from Franz Helm's *Buch von den Probierten Künsten*. 1535 'Two master gunners both armed with swords and one holding a linstock discussing whether it is the fire or the steam which forces the ball out of the cannon.' (Courtesy: University Library Heidelberg, Cod. Pal. germ. 128)
As the importance of the artillery steadily increased, so too did the standing of the master gunners. Their work, however, was distrusted and even considered sorcery and the devil's work.[13] However, the self-awareness of the master gunner and his personnel separated them from the rank-and-file landsknechts. They saw themselves as a guild requiring specialist knowledge and training and stood out from the common landsknecht in their clothing. Their fabrics and armour were more elaborate, the decorations of their hose more ornate, with dark colours, often black, preferred. Above all, however, they had privileges that only they, as members of the "artillery", enjoyed: no waiting in line for provisions, a separate camp kitchen away from cavalry and infantry, privileges of booty, special allowances for victories in the field the right to grant asylum and apply their own discipline and justice. Neither the commander of the horse nor the provost marshal (*Profoss*) had jurisdiction over them. They were solely under the jurisdiction of the master general of the ordnance (*Oberster Zeugmeister*).

---

13   Reinhard Baumann, *Landsknechte* (Munich: C.H. Beck Verlag. 1994), p.121.

Financing the Siege

Financing the siege from within his diocese proved to be a major challenge for the Bishop. The estates had decided that all churches and monasteries should hand over their treasures to the authorities lest they fall into the hands of the Anabaptists; however there was considerable resistance to the proposal. Nevertheless, the nobility, clergy and citizenry of the diocese had met in Telgte on 9 March and promised financial assistance in the fight against Münster. In total the sequestration of church assets yielded the sum of 12,298 guilders. In addition, all churches and monasteries in the diocese were to be subject to a 10 per cent levy on their annual income due on 4 May. This was calculated at 7,645 guilders. Again there was widespread resistance from the priories. On 1 May the authorities introduced, for the first time, a tax on property and livestock over and above a per capita income tax. The Bishop's accountants valued the property tax yield at 12,635 gold guilders, while the livestock valuation was estimated at 67,700 marks (Hanseatic). Many peasants resisted paying since they had been pressed into providing their labour for the Bishop's siegeworks.

Beyond taxation, the Bishop sought a number of private loans. At the Hiltrup regional assembly, which met on 17 March, a decision was made to take out short-term borrowing which the clergy of Münster would be expected to repay. Loans were acquired from Paderborn (2,100 guilders), Osnabrück (1,000 guilders), St Johanni-Osnabrück (100 guilders) the Cappenberg monastery (2,000 Guilders). A further 23,450 guilders were borrowed in April and May from numerous nobles and merchants in sums ranging from 100 to 8,000 guilders at a rate of interest between 5 per cent to 10 per cent. [14]

Negotiations with the Neighbouring Princes

Beyond his local efforts to raise finances, Bishop von Waldeck looked further afield for support. At the Imperial Diet at Speyer, neighbouring lords had pledged military support to each other in the event of any further popular uprisings. The Bishop had always maintained close relations with the Princes of Cologne, Cleves and Hessen, however, events within the Holy Roman Empire had begun to shake this alliance.

Landgrave Philipp von Hessen had taken a keen interest in the events in Münster during the years 1532–1533. His own foreign policy concerns were directed towards restricting the House of Habsburg, whose expulsion from Württemberg was imminent and whose influence through the House of Burgundy had spread to the Low Countries with monasteries at

---

14   Karl-Heinz Kirchhoff, 'Die Belagerung und Eroberung Münsters 1534/35' in *Westfälische Zeitschrift* volume 112 (1962), pp.84–87.

THE BISHOP'S SIEGE PREPARATIONS

Overyssel, Friesland, Groningen and Utrecht falling under Burgundian control. This had not been lost on the Princes of Cologne, Cleves and Guelders whose territories were threatened by this expansionist policy.

Rumours of a relationship between the Bishop and Burgundy had been circulating and prompted suspicion on the part of the neighbouring princes, which in turn led to a sluggishness in their responses to his call for military aid. For two months Bishop von Waldeck sought military aid from Cologne and Cleves. At the end of April, he sent a further delegation to Cologne with a request to the Archbishop to send sufficient artillery and troops to enable the construction of two more camps outside the city. The response was less than encouraging: the authorities in Cologne were surprised to learn that no assault had yet taken place and found it difficult to accept that the Bishop's forces were not strong enough to undertake this.[15]

3.9. Philipp, Landgraf von Hesse who provided Lutheran support to the Catholic Bishop. This stone relief dated 1542 is in the former Cistercian priory Haina in Hessen. (Public domain)

Aid From Hessen

The Bishop's request for support from Hessen came through, despite the Landgrave having his own plans for a military incursion into Württemberg. Both Philipp and Bishop von Waldeck shared the same political aims. At the end of April, the Bishop's envoy arrived in Kassel and in addition to a request for artillery, proposed that the Princes meet in Arolsen on 10 March. However, because the siege had already commenced, the Bishop had to cancel the meeting but requested financial support for his commander Wilken Steding to recruit mercenaries in Saxony.

In return for his support Philipp expected reciprocal military aid from the Bishop, and hoped to recruit horse for his own campaign once the siege was over. During his planned absence, the Landgraf expected the Bishop to defend Hessen. Upon agreement Philipp released two companies of men for a month and two cannon with a promise to extend this should the need arise. At the end of March, Hessen troops were the first 'outside' contingents to arrive at the Bishop's camps. A month earlier, the Bishop had sent one of his stewards, Cord Ketteler, to Düsseldorf with a request for the loan of six field guns from Herzog Johann von Cleves but met with the answer that the Herzog had ordered his officials not to support anyone from 'Münsterland'.

---

15 Hermann von Kerssenbroch, (Christopher S. Mackay tr.), *Narratio Historica Anabaptistici Furoris Monasterium*, (*Narrative of the Anabaptist Madness. The overthrow of Münster, the Famous Metropolis of Westphalia*) (Leiden–Boston: Brill 2007), p.528.

'A MIGHTY FORTRESS OF GOD': THE SIEGE OF MÜNSTER 1534-35

3.10. Johann III, Herzog von Jülich-Cleves-Berg known as Johann the Peaceful, was the Lord of Ravensberg, Count of Marck, and founder of the United Duchies of Jülich-Cleves-Berg. Johann adopted a stance of religious tolerance in the United Duchies but limited the circulation of Lutheran texts or teachings. He remained a Catholic throughout his life. (Public domain)

The artillery was forthcoming only after protracted negotiations.

The Bishop was concerned to build up his artillery park and amass sufficient finances in his war chest to continue the siege. His approaches to the Archbishop in Cologne and Cleves were met with ongoing suspicion and the officials of Cleves were suspicious of his true intentions with Münster, believing that following a successful siege he would hand the city over to Burgundy. Nevertheless, in the short term the threat posed by the Anabaptists was real enough for them and, at the meeting at Orsoy, they agreed to provide two companies of their own men on the proviso that any negotiations were to be undertaken in strict consultation with the Princes and their officials.

Both the Archbishop and the Herzog von Cleves sent cannon to the Bishop but the offered two companies never materialised. Similarly, the requested loan of 10,000 guilders made to the Archbishop was not fulfilled until the end of April and then only against collateral of several favourable properties within the diocese. The Bishop's failure to acquire full and unequivocal support from the Princes at the Orsoy meeting meant that he would still have to depend politically on both Hessen and Burgundy in his efforts to take Münster. Nevertheless, he returned the two companies of Hessen mercenaries after their period of service had run out on 19 April, given that he now had new recruits of his own who would be swearing their oath of allegiance to him instead of the Landgraf. He provided the Hessians with a letter of safe conduct.

3.11. Hermann von Wied (1477-1552), was Archbishop and Elector of Cologne from 1515 to 1547, as well as Prince-Bishop of Paderborn from 1532 to 1547. He unsuccessfully attempted to convert the archdiocese to Protestantism with the Cologne Reformation and resigned his offices in 1547. He is commemorated here on a medallion by the engraver Friedrich Hagenauer. (Münzkabinett, Staatliche Museen zu Berlin, Photo: Reinhard Saczewski Public Domain)

4

Initial Siege Efforts 1534

Chronology 1534

February	First Anabaptist sortie to destroy St Maurice's church
March	Initial raids on landsknecht camps undertaken
21–24 March	Netherlands authorities thwart a Melchiorite trek to Münster in Hasselt
5 April	(Easter Sunday) Jan Matthijs, leads a sortie from the city and is brutally killed by the Bishop's landsknechts
	Bishop's men approach the gates and taunt the Anabaptists
	Jan of Leiden assumes spiritual leadership
9 April	Church towers and steeples are destroyed in artillery bombardment
16 May	Münster carries out further sorties
25 May	(Whit Monday) First assault ends in failure
16 June	Failed attempt by Hille Feicken to assassinate the Bishop
20 June	Archbishop of Cologne and Herzog von Cleves offer additional financial support to the Bishop
June	Mutiny in the Meissen camp
	Offerkamp's failed 'ramp'
July	Meeting in Neuss to discuss continuing support for the siege
30 July	Leiden appeals to the Bishop's landsknechts
	Molleneck's failed uprising against the introduction of polygamy in the city
19 August	Council of War in Essen
25 August	Delegation enters the city to discuss surrender terms.
27 August	Bombardment of city begins
31 August	Second unsuccessful assault
1 September	Official coronation of Jan of Leiden as King of New Israel
	Commencement of the construction of the blockhouses

'A MIGHTY FORTRESS OF GOD': THE SIEGE OF MÜNSTER 1534-35

23 October	Anabaptist 'Apostles' are sent to neighbouring cities to garner support
2 November	Council of war decides to starve the city into submission
	The Bishop's emissary, Fabricius, is sent into the city to negotiate peace terms but is unsuccessful

The Bishop had laid plans to take the city as early as March. The plan was to have the outer moat drained in key places to facilitate an assault on the outer rampart and roundels at the city gates. Waldeck had asked his counterpart in Liège to send two hundred labourers to undermine the walls and ditches. However, because of a lack of manpower and firepower, preparation for the assault could not commence until the end of April. Moreover, considerable numbers of peasants had to be redeployed to the powder store at the village of Wolbeck to the southeast of the city which was under threat after repeated sorties by the Anabaptists.

For two months Waldeck sought to acquire military aid from Cologne and Cleves. At the end of April, he sent a further legation to Cologne with a request to the Archbishop to send sufficient artillery and troops to enable the construction of two more camps outside the city.

The Bishop was forced to mount his first assault using the troops he had at his disposal. He targeted the Jews' Field Gate because the access road did not go underneath the roundel but was adjacent to it. The outer moat that circled the roundel was particularly easy to drain at this point, as the land was 7 to 8 metres higher than the level of the River Aa. Protected by a battery of nine cannon, the bishop's peasants toiled for 5 days to dig an extended trench up to the gate. Under cover of darkness, some of his troops made an unsuccessful attempt at burning down the gatehouse at the roundel to prepare the way for the draining of the moat.[1]

From 29 April to 8 May around 300 peasants from the Wolbeck, Stromberg, Werne and Horstmar parishes – overseen by

4.1. The Siege of Budapest in 1541 by Erhard Schön. This woodcut is a good representation as to how contemporary siegeworks were set up.

---

[1] Karl-Heinz Kirchhoff, 'Die Belagerung und Eroberung Münsters 1534/35' in *Westfälische Zeitschrift* volume 112 (1962), pp.88–89.

INITIAL SIEGE EFFORTS 1534

their bailiffs and a group of 48 landsknechts – most probably Saxon miners – worked in four teams day and night, but after a week it became clear that the task was too great. On 10 May, a further 600 men from the parish of Emsland, and 400 from Cloppenburg were pressed into siege work. A week later the parishes of Vechta (500 men), Harpstedt, and Wildeshausen (300 men each) were called upon for their assistance.

Now, 1,000 workers were toiling daily to drain the moat by the Jews' Field Gate. After two weeks of frantic work the end was in sight. On 13 May, the Bishop gave the order for assault. There was to be a four day bombardment, and the assault was to begin on 19 May. On 15 May twelve wagons, pulled by about 100 horses, stood ready to transport munitions and siege equipment. Some 85 siege ladders had been fabricated in the Emsland. The master gunners commanding 35 siege cannon were ordered to fire 20 rounds each day on the city. The Bishop's horse was to be used as a second line of attack behind the infantry. Confidence was so high that the Landgraf Philipp von Hessen wrote to the King of Denmark that he expected the Bishop's mercenaries to be back on the open market within two weeks.

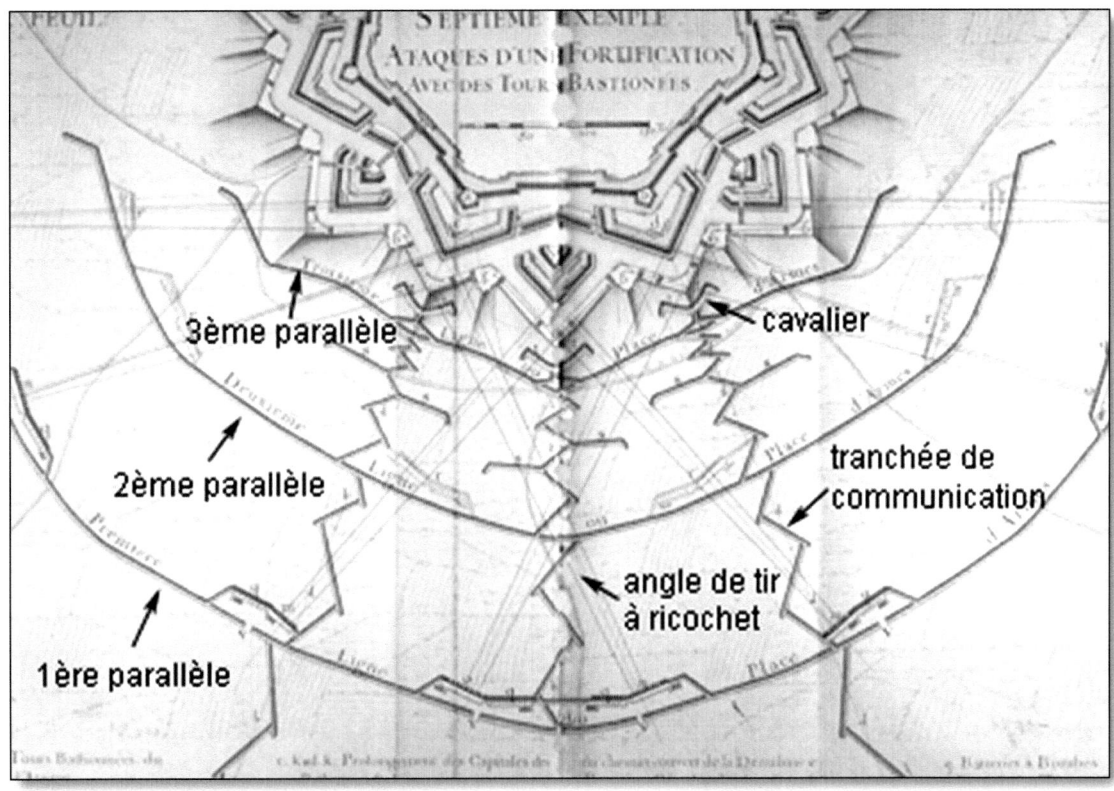

4.2. The trench system of siege parallels was in its infancy at this time and did not reach full fruition until the latter half of the seventeenth century under Sébastian, Marquis de Vauban. Three parallel trenches were dug in front of the walls, the earth excavated from them being used to create embankments screening the attackers from the defenders' fire, while bringing the attackers as close to the assault point as possible. Artillery was moved into the trenches, allowing it to target the base of the gatehouses with the defenders unable to depress their own guns enough to counter this move; once a breach had been made the city could then be stormed. The parallel trenches were linked by communication lines which zigzagged to avoid a straight line of fire.

On the eve of the assault a squad of men were tasked with filling the dry moat with brushwood fascines to provide a crossing point for the assaulting troops. However, on the night before the planned assault, a group of drunken mercenaries alerted the city defenders who managed to remove the fascines, forcing the planned assault to be called off. To make matters worse, a spiking raid was organised by the Anabaptists who, catching the watch off guard, descended on a gun emplacement:

> There were nineteen guns in the mantlets, and some of the townsmen fixed the steel nails in the small holes through which the fire is transmitted to the powder, others drove the nails home with the iron hammers, applying as much force as possible, and yet others cut up the wheels to the gun carriages and their emplacements with the axes, smashing, ruining and destroying everything to the extent allowed by time. Also finding gunpowder there, they scattered it all over the place across the sand …. When this slaughter was reported in the camps …. the troops burst forth in full force and pursued the townsmen, but they did not dare to advance closer than gunshot range through fear of the townsmen's crafty ingenuity. By provoking them, the townsmen led the soldiers, who were unaware of the trap, to the spot where the gunpowder was scattered over the sand, and immediately set light to it. At this point, the astonished soldiers standing in the middle of flames were horribly burned, and the rest of the soldiers stopped in terror at the very gruesome spectacle presented by their comrades.[2]

The episode was a major blow for the Prince Bishop who was forced to send an embarrassing report to the Landgraf von Hessen:

> We cannot conceal from you how, following 5 days of bombardment, we have decided with our officers and men to storm the city of Münster early in the morning [with] the hope of taking the city, or at least the outer rampart. However, we have to report that some drunken landsknechts mounted an attack last night at 11 o'clock, without the order and knowledge of our commanders, and were beaten back by the city dwellers with some 200 dead and wounded on our side …. thus preventing us from mounting our planned assault …. Be that as it may, with God's help we will continue our

---

2   Hermann von Kerssenbroch, (Christopher S. Mackay tr.), *Narratio Historica Anabaptistici Furoris Monasterium*, (*Narrative of the Anabaptist Madness. The overthrow of Münster, the Famous Metropolis of Westphalia*) (Leiden–Boston: Brill 2007), p.559.

INITIAL SIEGE EFFORTS 1534

4.3. Wheelbarrow - used in sieges to carry, earth, gunpowder, and cannon balls. (Drawing by Geoff Laws based on a surviving example in the Bayerisches Armeemuseum in Ingoldstadt)

cause in earnest, confident that we will bring the city of Münster to heel.[3]

After the first failed attempt to take the city, numbers of mercenaries had left the camp. It would be difficult to mount a swift assault and the outer ditch still needed to be filled in before assessing the feasibility of any renewed attack. Working through the night, the Bishop's sappers were able to establish entrenchments and gun emplacements in front of the Cross Gate and the St Maurice Gate. To further this work, the Bishop made an approach to the town of Ysselstein to acquire the military engineer, Hans Franke.

On 2 June, the Council of War carried out an inspection. It was decided to mount a renewed assault only once the outer moat had been drained. Some displaced citizens from Münster who were familiar with the lie of the land were brought in and advised that it would be possible to drain off the water at several designated locations within about 4 to 5 days. There was however doubt within the Bishop's council of war regarding the chances of success of a frontal assault. A consensus was beginning to form that blockhouses should be built to encircle the city and starve the Anabaptists into submission. Others wanted to set fire to the city.

On 3 June, the Bishop ordered all the peasants of the abbey who were liable to serve to be mustered for work. The peasants were to work for ten days, the townspeople for three weeks. But before the first contingent could start work, the plan proved to be impracticable. The troops manning the city walls made it impossible to get close enough to the trench. One of the Bishop's siege engineers, Gerd Offerkamp, proposed a new plan for a huge earthen rampart to be erected towards the outer defences of the city between the Hörster and St Maurice gates. Known as *Die Grosse Graft*[4] it was to be raised in the empty fields and gradually extended by the efforts of the

---

3   Letter dated 26 May 1534. cf Richard van Dülmen, *Das Täuferreich zu Münster 1534-1535: Berichte und Dokumente* (Munich Deutscher Taschenbuch Verlag, 1974), p.133. (Author's translation)
4   This word no longer used in German but from it may come the English slang word 'graft', with its meaning of to work hard.

'A MIGHTY FORTRESS OF GOD': THE SIEGE OF MÜNSTER 1534-35

4.4. This section of the camp of Karl V at Lauingen gives an idea of how the infantry camps may have appeared during the earlier part of the siege. (Photo: Hermann Mueller, courtesy Heimathaus, Stadt Lauingen)

peasants in the direction of the city so that the moat could be filled in. The result would be that once any difficulty in scaling the walls was removed, the soldiers would have no trouble in spreading out in an extended battle formation to enter the city.

Kerssenbroch describes the principle as follows:

> They (the sappers) were to come equipped with knapsacks on their shoulders containing sustenance for three days and with shovels for digging and piling up dirt. During the night, a small, low mound was raised between the Horst Gate and the Gate of St Maurice at just about gunshot range, and with the large amount of dirt that was piled up by the peasants' constant efforts this mound became larger and taller. Offerkamp, who was in charge of this operation, arranged the peasants in ranks of three, four, five or more according to the height of the pile. In this way, the diggers in the lowest rank would quickly pick up dirt from the base of the mound and heave it to the

second and so on, with the lower diggers always passing it on to the next rank. The top rank would throw the dirt given to them by the lower rank onto the top of the mound, always making sure that a sufficient height of the mound remained above them to cover their bodies, so that gunfire from the town would not harm them.[5]

Although some disagreed, most commanders judged that Offerkamp's plan offered a useful method of shortening the war and the Bishop's authorization was quickly secured. In early June detailed orders were issued for all peasants capable of work to be pressed into service. 2,800 men from six districts in the upper bishopric were mustered, a further 265 from fourteen small towns on 8 June, and a contingent of 2,600 from five districts of the upper bishopric on 13 June. Finally, some 3,800 from six districts of the lower bishopric received an order on 14 June. Many men were reluctant to comply, and further demands were made of five districts on 23 June and of five more the following day. Several thousand men were also mustered in Bishop von Waldeck's other bishoprics of Minden and Osnabrück.

4.5. Offerkamp's *Graft*. See text for description. (Diagram by the author)

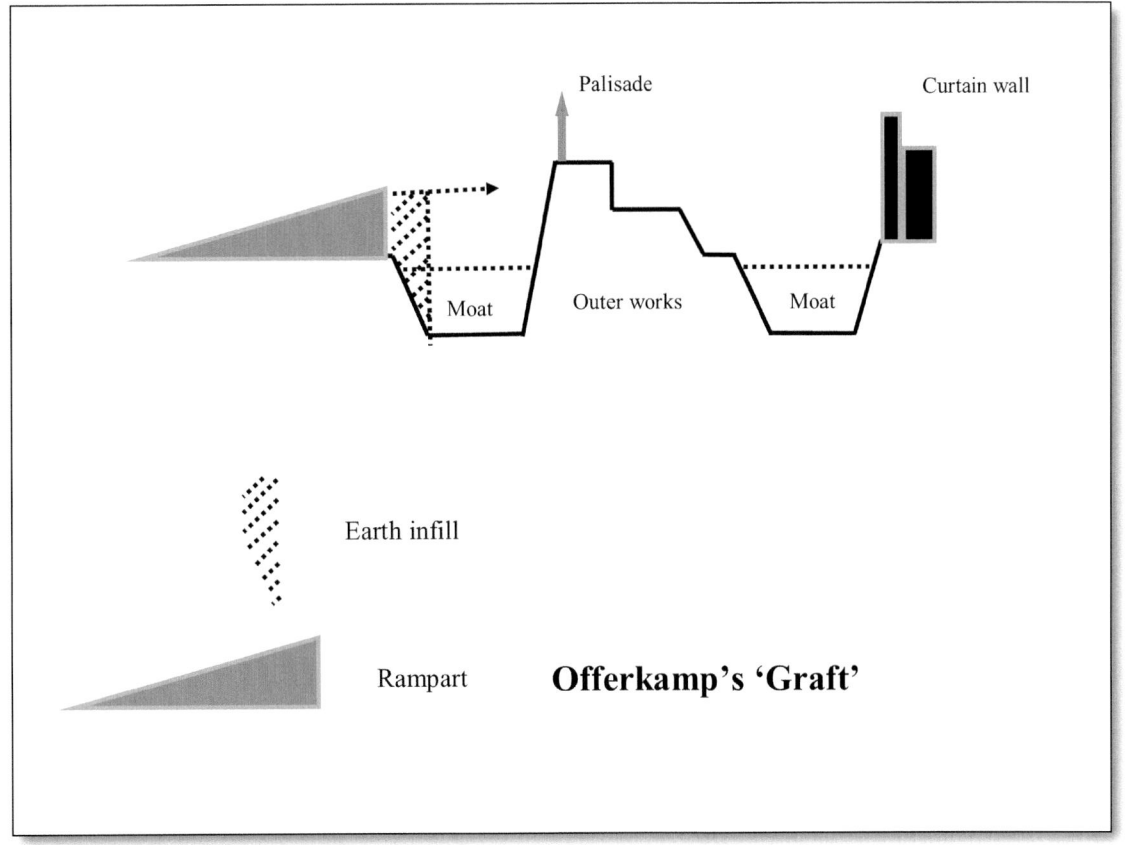

---

5   Hermann von Kerssenbroch, (Christopher S. Mackay tr.), *Narratio Historica Anabaptistici Furoris Monasterium*, (*Narrative of the Anabaptist Madness. The overthrow of Münster, the Famous Metropolis of Westphalia*) (Leiden–Boston: Brill 2007), p.561.

'A MIGHTY FORTRESS OF GOD': THE SIEGE OF MÜNSTER 1534-35

He ordered that for the work to be done, the peasants of the diocese were to be organised into gangs so that they could be summoned to work in relays. The Bishop's sappers 'grafted' through most of the summer and Offerkamp's raised rampart rolled forward towards the outer work as the furthest rank of sappers threw dirt down into the moat.

In addition to the portable wooden mantlets which offered some protection to the sappers, the Bishop's mercenaries were ordered to set up 'redoubts' of stacked bundles of brushwood at night, from which good marksmen with hook guns could provide some covering fire. Progress with the rampart was slow so that even by the end of July, it was expected to take another three months to reach the city's outer rampart. This enormous undertaking was going to require more men and the Bishop decided to also call on Cologne and Cleves to press their subjects into the task. Despite resistance from various quarters, several thousand additional labourers could be mustered so that progress with the ramp could proceed at some pace.

> ## Mutiny in the Meissen camp.
>
> A group of Meissen landsknechts based at the camp before St Tilgen's Gate abandoned their positions at night on the last day of June. This was mutiny, punishable by death under the landsknecht disciplinary code. When news reached the Bishop, he immediately ordered Bernard von Westerholt, the commander in chief of the cavalry, to pursue them with a detachment of his men. Von Westerholt caught up with the mercenaries to the south-east of the city close to the town of Sendenhorst where they had ensconced themselves in a fortified manor. The Meissen landsknechts, who were well armed with pikes and arquebuses, had thrown up improvised defences in anticipation of an assault by the Bishop's men-at-arms. Led by Derek von Recke and his brother, the cavalry charged the gate and managing to remove it from its hinges, paving the way for the assault. However, both were mortally wounded by gun fire and the Bishop's horse was forced to beat a retreat and sent word for firepower to be brought up to assist. When the reinforcements arrived, including a light field piece, the deserters laid down their arms and surrendered, giving the Bishop the discretion either to pardon or to execute them. They were brought back from Sendenhorst to Wolbeck where they were imprisoned in the church. The Bishop passed them over to the officers, sergeants, and the rank and file for judgement. Declared to be, 'disloyal, wicked, disgraceful oath-breakers and sentenced to be pardoned or punished by the Prince .... they made no end of entreating him .... the Prince was moved and after punishing those responsible for the desertion and flight, he mitigated his previous decision with lenient mercy and forgave the rest.'[6]

---

6   Hermann von Kerssenbroch, (Christopher S. Mackay tr.), *Narratio Historica Anabaptistici Furoris Monasterium*, (*Narrative of the Anabaptist Madness. The overthrow of Münster, the Famous Metropolis of Westphalia*) (Leiden–Boston: Brill 2007), p. 618.

At the beginning of August, it was certain that the outer moat would be bridged by the end of the month. One last push was necessary. Once again "the third man" was to be mustered in eight parishes to work from 12 August to 31 August. The erection of the *Graft* put an enormous strain on the Bishop's war chest so that by the end of the month he felt once again compelled to approach his neighbouring states for financial support.

4.6. A number of outlandish siege devices were imagined at the time, none more so than by Franz Helm in *Kriegsbuch* involving birds and animals with explosive charges attached to their bodies:

> Create a small sack like a fire-arrow …. if you would like to get at a town or castle, seek to obtain a cat from that place. And bind the sack to the back of the cat, ignite it, let it glow well and thereafter let the cat go, so it runs to the nearest castle or town, and out of fear it thinks to hide itself where it ends up in barn hay or straw it will be ignited.

(Source: 'Buch der probierten Künsten', f.74r. Courtesy: Universitätsbibliothek Heidelberg)

The Anabaptist defenders were astute in their response to the erection of Offerkamp's ramp. They began by building mounds of earth on top of the outer works reinforcing these with beams and stone statues plundered from sarcophagi out of several of the city's churches, but these mounds were constructed in such a way as to leave passageways and tunnels underneath. On the mounds they planted sharpened stakes pointing downwards to ward off any assault from below.

As Kerssenbroch describes:

Pretending not to notice, the townsmen put up with this for some time in order that their lack of response would entice the enemy closer and within gunshot range. Thinking that this harm was no longer to be tolerated, they first placed heavy artillery opposite Offerkamp's mound and used it to shake loose what was often a large amount of stones, which then scattered over the peasants. Then, from the oblique bulwarks and newly raised mounds they fired such a quantity of shot that no one was able to stand on top of the raised roadway and virtually no shot fired from the higher ground was in vain. With some killed, some wounded and others knocked down from the new construction, Offerkamp's plan not only bore no fruit …. it wore out the peasants with vast toil and expenses, bringing death to many…⁷

In addition, the defenders sought to undermine the efforts of the Bishop's sappers by taking out of the moat at night whatever the sappers had thrown in during the day. However, they were unable to keep this up for long as Gresbeck records:

They did this in the city for three or four nights. Eventually, the Bishop's men threw in so much that they could no longer remove it and gave up taking it out at night.⁸

There was an ongoing firefight during much of this work with the defenders making slings to throw boulders at the sappers as they sought to fill in the moat. If a landsknecht or peasant sapper exposed himself, he would be immediately shot at, attracting return fire from those landsknechts positioned near the top of the ramp in order to provide covering fire.⁹

By the end of July, the war funding agreed at Neuss had been used up and at the beginning of August the Bishop's landsknechts had not received any pay for a week. On 5 August, the Archbishop of Cologne arrived in the camp to consult with Bishop von Waldeck and the war councils on 'measures that should bring victory.' Widening the participation of the nobility seemed advisable, especially since the Westphalian estates had shown little inclination to contribute. The Bishop wrote to the Emperor Ferdinand, the Electors of Mainz, Trier, Saxony, and Brandenburg, the Herzogs von Brunswick, von Lüneburg and von Saxony, to the Bishop of Liège and to Landgraf Philipp for support in the fight against the dangerous uprising in Münster. The response was overwhelmingly negative – only the Landgraf responded positively with a substantial sum of money and 20 tons of powder while the Graf von Rhineland Palatinate offered 50 hundredweight of gunpowder. The Bishop had half expected this, requesting on 13 August, that the Cleves contingents ask for further assistance. By now the siege had cost him over 450,000 guilders, in the last month alone some 45,000 guilders for his landsknechts and 30,000 for the cannon. Once again Cologne and

---

7   Hermann von Kerssenbroch, (Christopher S. Mackay tr.), *Narratio Historica Anabaptistici Furoris Monasterium*, (*Narrative of the Anabaptist Madness. The overthrow of Münster, the Famous Metropolis of Westphalia*) (Leiden–Boston: Brill 2007), p.562.
8   Heinrich Gresbeck (Christopher S. Mackay trans. and added commentary), *False Prophets and Preachers: Henry Gresbeck's Account of the Anabaptist Kingdom of Münster* (Kirksville: Truman State University Press 2016), p.107.
9   Heinrich Gresbeck (Christopher S. Mackay trans. and added commentary), *False Prophets and Preachers: Henry Gresbeck's Account of the Anabaptist Kingdom of Münster* (Kirksville: Truman State University Press 2016), p.107.

INITIAL SIEGE EFFORTS 1534

Cleves were prepared to provide financial assistance to prevent a mutiny before the planned assault. On 19 August, at a meeting in Essen they agreed two immediate further loans of 20,000 and 5,000 Emden guilders, and a further 22,500 in the following week in order that the mercenaries could be relied upon to mount the second assault.

In the meantime, the entrenchment work had been partially successful. At the Jews' Field Gate, the outer moat had been cut and drained and work had begun to fill it in. At the Hörster Gate, Offerkamp's *Graft* had advanced to the moat, but defensive fire had driven the sappers back again and again, rendering the filling of the moat almost impossible. The Bishop summoned all the military officers to a council of war on 24 August. The Archbishop of Cologne, the Count Palatine, the Herzog von Grubenhagen, the Grafs von Schauenburg, Isenburg, Nassau, Waldeck, Neuenahr, Oberstein, Bentheim and Wied, and many other members of the knighthood were in attendance. There was considerable debate about the ongoing siegeworks. Digging had ground to a halt because the trenches and moats were once again under water. Nevertheless, it was decided to mount an assault should planned negotiations fail. Under the promise of a safe conduct, both sides granted a three hours' truce, and a delegation entered the city on 25 August. Although the subject concerned all the citizens, the delegates were only permitted to meet Jan van Leiden and a small entourage. Under the offer of clemency for all, the Anabaptists were expected to repent their impious rebellion and surrender to the Bishop. If, on the other hand, they were not prepared to entertain the proposals, the city would face an assault by the might of the besieging army.

After the Anabaptists rejected the call to surrender on 25 August, a four day barrage from four sides of the city began on 27 August.

> The fearsome thundering of the artillery could be heard clearly for more than sixteen Westphalian miles, and in the more adjacent country districts and manors, the windowpanes were either shaken from their housings or smashed when the lead was wrenched loose by the constant shaking. Many city gates were cast down when the framework holding them together was broken apart. Some of them hung there tottering and threatened to fall to the ground, and these the townsmen pulled back with ropes to keep them from collapsing into the ditches. The towers rising upon the walls were knocked in with shells, and they caved in and threw down the men occupying them. Since much slaughter had been inflicted on the men from Guelders with gunfire from the tower of the Church of St Mary, much effort and cost was vainly spent in the attempt to knock this tower down. It has a very strong base solidly constructed of local marble and quite firm mortar, so it readily spat back any hits made

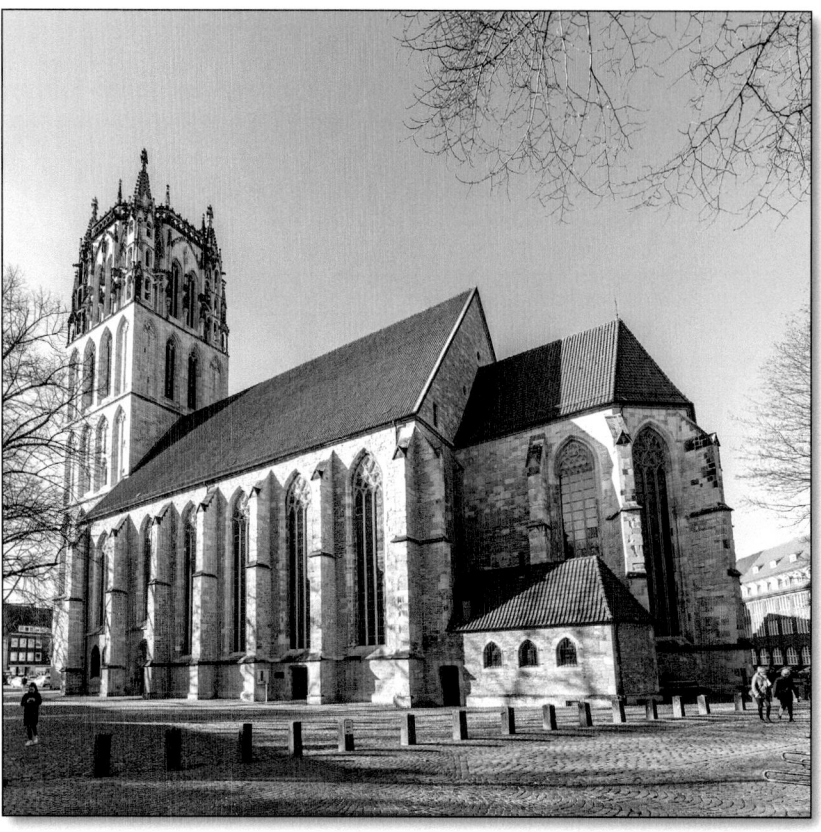

4.7. Officially titled St Marien Überwasser, dedicated to St Mary, the church had its spire and the baptismal font destroyed during the Münster rebellion. The flattened tower could serve as a position from which the Anabaptists were able to bombard the Guelders camp which made it a target during the second assault. (Photo: Mathias Süßen via Wikimedia Commons)

by the artillery, though its summit had chunks knocked out of it on the west side to no effect.[10]

On the morning of 31 August, the assault on the city gates began. It had been agreed that the signal for attack would be the firing of *The Devil*, Phillip von Hessen's enormous cannon – to be fired at 5 a.m. The roar would be heard across all the infantry camps.[11] As the drummers gave the sound to arms,

---

10 Hermann von Kerssenbroch, (Christopher S. Mackay tr.), *Narratio Historica Anabaptistici Furoris Monasterium*, (*Narrative of the Anabaptist Madness. The overthrow of Münster, the Famous Metropolis of Westphalia*) (Leiden–Boston: Brill 2007), pp.673–674.

11 The council of war had decided that the princes, counts, barons and members of the knighthood who were the highest officers should stay out of the assault and maintain positions away from the affray. If, however, the assault was repulsed, then the main columns should be reinforced by the horse and where necessary they

the ensigns and sergeants marshalled their men to rush for the city from six directions. However, on the day of the assault all the trenches still stood under water rendering a concerted attack difficult. Kerssenbroch reports that the landsknechts dumped a number of carts along with their loads of osier, bundles of wood, straw, and broom into the moat. Some men crossed by leaning down on the wicker mantlets, using their swords to hack open those wooden mantlets which the defenders had installed as makeshift barricades on the ramparts. Others fixed hooked ladders to the remains of the smashed gates and climbed up. Some squads endeavoured to blow gates off their hinges with gunpowder charges. Some ensigns stood on top of the walls to direct their men below.[12]

Once they realized that the landsknechts were about to storm the city, the defenders took up position on the walls deploying all the women, young and old at their positions on the outer works. As Gresbeck describes:

> …they had made preparations for the assault by boiling water with lime and making tar (pitch) wreaths and equipping themselves with artillery, and with everything just as if they considered it a matter of life or death.[13]

The landsknechts launched two assaults outside each gate, but at some gates they launched three. At the New Bridge and Cross Gates, the defenders allowed the enemy to pass the first ditch and rampart as if they had deserted their positions. When the rear ranks of the landsknecht column saw this, they thought that their 'forlorn hope' had made it into the city and pressed forward. The Anabaptist defenders however were lying in wait ready to ambush the attackers from their concealed positions in the bulwarks. When they thought that enough enemy troops had crossed the rampart, they opened fire on them from above with the arquebuses sounding, 'just like herring eggs thrown into a fire, crackling without stop.'[14] Such was

---

should dismount in order to urge the infantry forward by example. In addition, the cavalry brought in after the capture was to refrain from plundering. Instead, they were to retain the cohesion of their units and follow their commanders. Hermann von Kerssenbroch, (Christopher S. Mackay tr.), *Narratio Historica Anabaptistici Furoris Monasterium*, (*Narrative of the Anabaptist Madness. The overthrow of Münster, the Famous Metropolis of Westphalia*) (Leiden–Boston: Brill 2007), p.601.

12 Hermann von Kerssenbroch, (Christopher S. Mackay tr.), *Narratio Historica Anabaptistici Furoris Monasterium*, (*Narrative of the Anabaptist Madness. The overthrow of Münster, the Famous Metropolis of Westphalia*) (Leiden–Boston: Brill 2007), p.606.

13 *Heinrich Gresbeck* (Christopher S. Mackay trans. and added commentary), *False Prophets and Preachers: Henry Gresbeck's Account of the Anabaptist Kingdom of Münster* (Kirksville: Truman State University Press 2016), p.132.

14 *Heinrich Gresbeck* (Christopher S. Mackay trans. and added commentary), *False Prophets and Preachers: Henry Gresbeck's Account of the Anabaptist Kingdom of Münster* (Kirksville: Truman State University Press 2016), p.607.

'A MIGHTY FORTRESS OF GOD': THE SIEGE OF MÜNSTER 1534-35

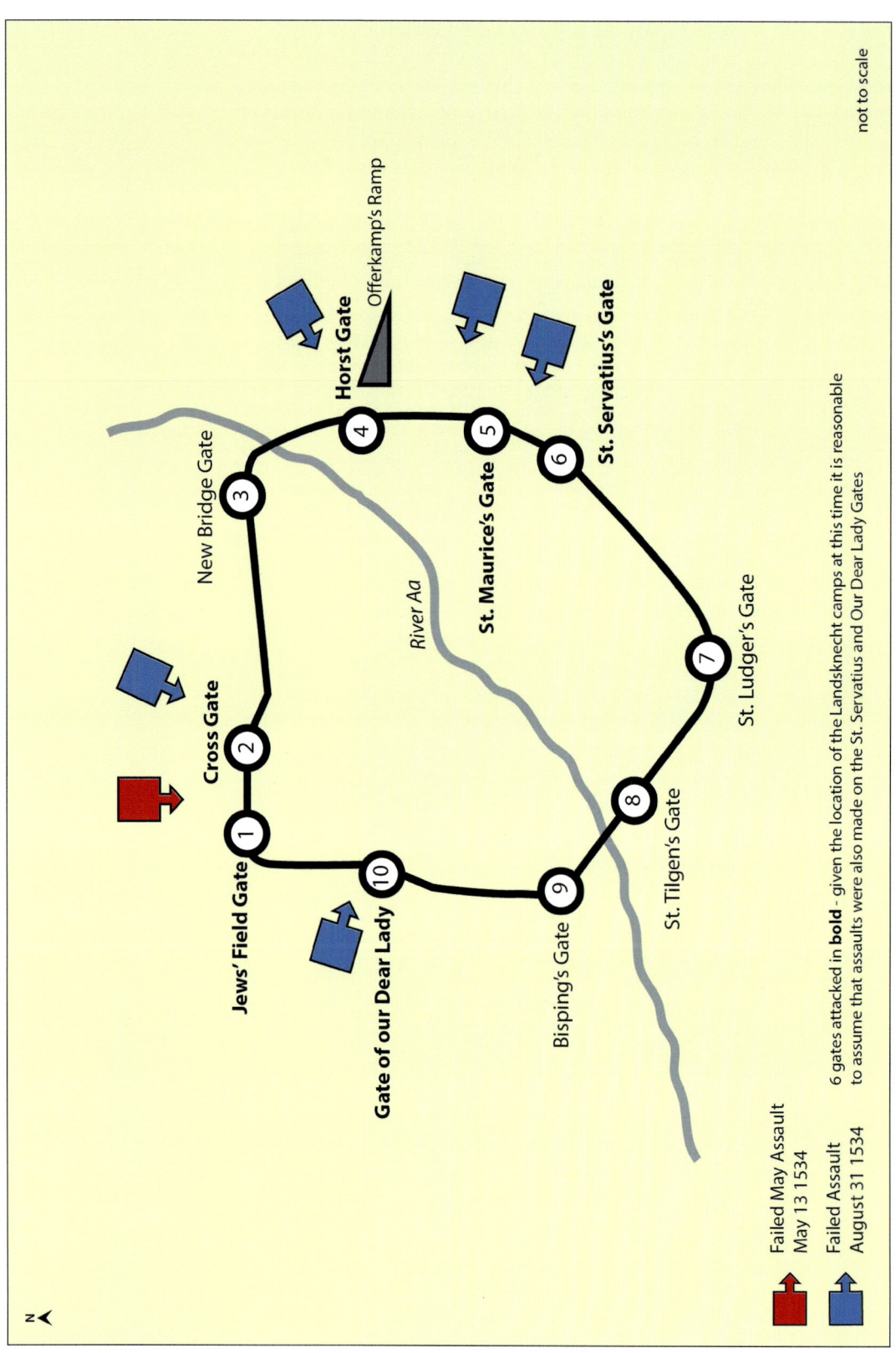

M.4. The failed assaults of 1534.

the ferocity of the Anabaptist defence of the outer fortifications that the Bishop's landsknechts were forced to retreat:

> Thrown back in this way, they often renewed the attack with fresh strength at the urging of the cavalry, and they vainly carried on with great losses until dusk. Eventually the survivors, who had been worn out by the length of the assault and were almost faint with fatigue and exhausted by their wounds, saw that not just the walls and ramparts but also the water in the ditches and the fields were red with the blood of their comrades, and that their bodies were scattered everywhere, (and) gave up all hope of taking the city.[15]

---

15   Heinrich Gresbeck (Christopher S. Mackay trans. and added commentary), *False Prophets and Preachers: Henry Gresbeck's Account of the Anabaptist Kingdom of Münster* (Kirksville: Truman State University Press 2016), p.607.

5

The Defence of the City 1534

Since the Middle Ages larger cities had drawn up their own military constitution or defence ordinance (*Wehrverfassung*), the prerequisite for which was the military sovereignty acquired in the mid-thirteenth century.[1] This included, above all, power over the city's fortifications, the right to enlist the citizenry into (compulsory) military service, the right to raise its own troops (*landsknechte*), and the freedom to enter into military alliances. Furthermore, the preservation of the right of occupation, safe passage and recruitment were all granted. External signs of military sovereignty were, inter alia, the right to bear a municipal banner and to prescribe a 'uniform' and specific weaponry.[2] In peacetime, supreme command would be vested in the municipal council, although the keeper of the arsenal (*Zeugmeister*) could enjoy a certain independence by dint of his expertise. One essential element of the ordinance concerned the establishment of a permanent city guard which might have to involve the hiring of mercenaries. Additional matters for decision were the regulation of the production of weapon stocks by the gun foundry, armoury and powder mill, and the stockpiling of these weapons in the city's arsenal.

The news that the Bishop was to lay siege to the city required a new ordinance in Münster. Estimates vary widely as to how many people stayed and how many departed from the city on 27 February. One estimate has around 2,000 emigrations occurring before the siege began, including both voluntary and compulsory. Between 5,000 and 5,500 of the original native population remained – 800 to 1,000 men, 3,000 to 3,300 women and 1,200 children. To this number must be added 700 to 800 men and about 1,500 women, predominantly, Dutch immigrants. The total besieged population

---

1. Hiram Kümper, 'Regimen von der Wehrverfassung: Ein Kriegsmemorandum aus der Gießener Handschrift 996, zugleich ein Beitrag zur städtischen Militärgeschichte des 15. Jahrhunderts., *Berichte und Arbeiten aus der Universitätsbibliothek und dem Universitätsarchiv, Gießen 55,* (Gießen: University 2005).
2. Klaus Militzer, 'Die Bewaffnung der Bürger West Deutscher Städte im Spätmittelalter' in *Fasciculi Archaeologiae Historicae*, Fase. XI.1998.

numbered thus about 7,500; of these between 1,500 and 1,800 men capable of bearing arms, and a further 4,700 men and women, as well as 200 children, all of whom were available to undertake some aspect of defence work.[3]

Following a rousing speech to the citizens,[4] mayor Knipperdolling organised the city's defence beginning with the appointment of officers, sergeants, and other leaders to put the populace on a war footing. Interestingly, according to Gresbeck, at the outset the Anabaptists eschewed the idea of having a fifer and drummer and ensigns in the ranks – this being viewed as ungodly. Eventually such puritanical sensibilities had to give way to military pragmatism given the significance of the '*Spiel*' in signalling specific deployments and formations.[5]

Having organised the citizenry into companies and squads (*Rotten*), a rota was established for keeping the watches day and night. Councillors were not excluded from the task.[6] The watch was rigorously patrolled and enforced by six special officers, so-called *Gewaltmeister*, who were occasionally accompanied by the mayor and city councillors.[7] Everyone was allotted a specific position in the city's defences and expected to hold this to the death to avoid any weakening of positions during any assault on different parts of the citadel. Münster enjoyed a well-stocked arsenal with 86 pieces of artillery, mainly culverins and demi culverins and falconets,[8] and over 450 heavy arquebuses positioned throughout its fortifications.

On 13 June, the elders ordered by common decision that 600 old men, schoolmasters, tailors, carpenters, blacksmiths, shoemakers, tanners, fishermen, bakers, brewers, butchers, and those entrusted with the administration of official jobs should be exempted and freed from the obligation to serve on the watch. On 17 June, they selected the four most experienced surgeons – Nicholas of Luxemburg, Albert of Sneek, Conrad

---

3   Willem De Bakker, Michael Driedger and James Stayer, *Bernhard Rothmann and the Reformation in Münster, 1530-35* (Kitchener: Pandora Press 2009), p.157.

4   Hermann von Kerssenbroch, (Christopher S. Mackay tr.), *Narratio Historica Anabaptistici Furoris Monasterium,* (*Narrative of the Anabaptist Madness. The overthrow of Münster, the Famous Metropolis of Westphalia*) (Leiden–Boston: Brill 2007), p.553.

5   Heinrich Gresbeck (Christopher S. Mackay trans. and added commentary), *False Prophets and Preachers: Henry Gresbeck's Account of the Anabaptist Kingdom of Münster* (Kirksville: Truman State University Press 2016), p.105.

6   Heinrich Gresbeck (Christopher S. Mackay trans. and added commentary), *False Prophets and Preachers: Henry Gresbeck's Account of the Anabaptist Kingdom of Münster* (Kirksville: Truman State University Press 2016), p.105.

7   Heinrich Gresbeck (Christopher S. Mackay trans. and added commentary), *False Prophets and Preachers: Henry Gresbeck's Account of the Anabaptist Kingdom of Münster* (Kirksville: Truman State University Press 2016), pp.71–72.

8   Karl-Heinz Kirchhoff, 'Die Belagerung und Eroberung Münsters 1534/35' in *Westfälische Zeitschrift* volume 112 (1962), p.83. See Jonathan Davies, *The Art of Shooting Great Ordinance* (Warwick: Helion & Co., 2022) for a discussion of artillery types.

Noest, and Matthew of Jülich to look after the wounded. They were to tend to the wounds by consulting with and assisting one another, but the sick were offered the right to ask for whichever surgeon they wanted.

The Anabaptists worked frantically to erect earthwork mounds in front of each gatehouse:

> For the foundations of these mounds, they used the sarcophagi of bishops, canons, noblemen, priests, and matrons and the polished flagstones which they had dug out of churches, and propped these up on the inner side with wood which they had seized all over the place with no regard for the property owners…[9]

Some of these improvised fortifications contained concealed underground tunnels and passageways with guns.[10]

Knipperdolling felt confident enough to announce to the citizens that nothing was wanting so far as the ability of the city to defend itself was concerned. There was a plentiful supply of powder and shot[11] and an 'abundance of lead in the roofs of churches and towers to cast them from.' The mayor was also confident in respect of supplies and financial resources in the form of both gold and silver.[12] The siege conditions provided even further justification for the Anabaptist principle of 'community of goods' by which all citizens were expected to give up their property. Supplies, in this case the store of communal property including foodstuffs, was henceforth to be managed by appointed deacons in each parish.[13]

Special defensive tasks were created with certain individuals equipped with fresh cattle hides and leather pitchers for smothering or extinguishing any fires caused by the enemy's projectiles. A separate detachment was

---

9 Hermann von Kerssenbroch, (Christopher S. Mackay tr.), *Narratio Historica Anabaptistici Furoris Monasterium*, (*Narrative of the Anabaptist Madness. The overthrow of Münster, the Famous Metropolis of Westphalia*) (Leiden–Boston: Brill 2007), p.591.

10 Hermann von Kerssenbroch, (Christopher S. Mackay tr.), *Narratio Historica Anabaptistici Furoris Monasterium*, (*Narrative of the Anabaptist Madness. The overthrow of Münster, the Famous Metropolis of Westphalia*) (Leiden–Boston: Brill 2007), p.528.

11 According to Gresbeck: They made powder in the city day and night in two oil mills and the old cathedral. *Heinrich Gresbeck* (Christopher S. Mackay trans. and added commentary), *False Prophets and Preachers: Henry Gresbeck's Account of the Anabaptist Kingdom of Münster* (Kirksville: Truman State University Press 2016), p.98.

12 Hermann von Kerssenbroch, (Christopher S. Mackay tr.), *Narratio Historica Anabaptistici Furoris Monasterium*, (*Narrative of the Anabaptist Madness. The overthrow of Münster, the Famous Metropolis of Westphalia*) (Leiden–Boston: Brill 2007), p.521.

13 *Heinrich Gresbeck* (Christopher S. Mackay trans. and added commentary), *False Prophets and Preachers: Henry Gresbeck's Account of the Anabaptist Kingdom of Münster* (Kirksville: Truman State University Press 2016), pp.82–85.

established to rapidly respond to any weak points in the city defences that were in danger of being breached. There was a team allocated the task of carrying powder to the gun emplacements. To support the arquebusiers on the outer works, boys were trained in the skill of sharpshooting. Women, who outnumbered the 1,500 men by three to one, were given the task of heating lime and pitch on the ramparts, and some were also employed with weaving wreaths fashioned out of linen and oakum for dipping in flaming pitch to repel the enemy as they scaled the walls.

Beyond organising the defence of the city, from the outset the Anabaptists were particularly astute in deploying tactics which took the fighting to the besiegers. This they did in a number of ways: from carrying out raids, deploying snipers, spiking the Bishop's artillery, fouling the trenchworks and spreading propaganda, through to sanctioning an assassination attempt on the Bishop.

On 28 February Bishop von Waldeck initiated the blockade ordering the creation of infantry and cavalry camps at key strategic locations around the city. This did not deter the besieged from launching a series of raids. Using the many secret passageways into and out of the city, such raids would be made in groups of two, three, four or more, and at their discretion, would either fight the besiegers or escape their notice and bypass the camps and bring back supplies that they had either bought or seized in local villages.[14] Such raids were often undertaken under cover of darkness with each marauder wearing an overshirt as an identifying mark.[15]

5.1. Pitch wreaths or *Pechkränze* served to set alight the combustible parts of positions and of entrenchments, but also the attackers themselves. They were used by defenders and attackers alike. The pitch wreath, of a diameter between 19.5cm and 30 cm, consisted of a braided ring of string or willow, which had previously been treated with saltpetre. This would be dipped in different mixes of liquid pitch and gunpowder. Depending on the mixture they could explode or burned slowly. They were often difficult to extinguish. (Rendering: Geoff Laws)

As early as 25 February the Anabaptists undertook a pre-emptive strike to destroy St Maurice Church which lay just beyond the outer wall to the east of the city. The church would have provided a favourable position from which to bombard the city's defences, so it was necessary to reduce it to rubble. On 6 March, exiting through the Horst Gate, they burned down two

---

14   Hermann von Kerssenbroch, (Christopher S. Mackay tr.), *Narratio Historica Anabaptistici Furoris Monasterium*, (*Narrative of the Anabaptist Madness. The overthrow of Münster, the Famous Metropolis of Westphalia*) (Leiden–Boston: Brill 2007), p.667.
15   *Heinrich Gresbeck* (Christopher S. Mackay trans. and added commentary), *False Prophets and Preachers: Henry Gresbeck's Account of the Anabaptist Kingdom of Münster* (Kirksville: Truman State University Press 2016), p.101.

5.2. The church of the collegiate monastery of St Mauritz was considered the most important monastery in the diocese of Münster after the cathedral chapter of St Paul's Cathedral. In 1529, Bernhard Rothmann, the church's chaplain, began to preach in the Reformation. Thus, the monastery became the starting point of the development towards the Anabaptist Kingdom of Münster. After the Anabaptists gained control of the city in 1534, parts of the church were destroyed to prevent the Bishop from using it to bombard the city. (Photo: Chris06 via Wikimedia Commons)

mills and caused a number of casualties amongst the Bishop's mercenaries. On 13 March, in full daylight they set fire to two manors in the Jews' Field. In this skirmish, the city defenders lost thirty-five of their own men, but this did not prevent them from launching an even bolder raid the following day when a column numbering about 500 men sallied out at 10 o'clock in the morning and burned down the Potterhaus along with some brick huts. Almost cut off when the bishop's mercenaries attacked them from all sides, they were able to beat a retreat though a route unknown to their attackers. During this withdrawal, they captured an enemy drummer, cut off his head and hung it and his drum from the top of the Bischoping Gate as a provocative act of defiance.[16]

---

16   Heinrich Gresbeck (Christopher S. Mackay trans. and added commentary), *False Prophets and Preachers: Henry Gresbeck's Account of the Anabaptist Kingdom of Münster* (Kirksville: Truman State University Press 2016), p.555.

THE DEFENCE OF THE CITY 1534

> ## Snipers
>
> Unlike their landsknecht enemy, the city defenders were under strict orders to remain sober which often worked to their advantage in some of the exchanges of gunfire:
>
> > Bernard Buxdorp, a very daring man, often left the city alone armed with a triple handgun,[17] always just about at noon, and would challenge the quite drunken soldiers. Being made more daring in pursuing him through drink and acting incautiously, they would be cut down by the sober Buxdorp. He virtually let no day pass without shooting some soldiers. When he saw many soldiers rushing at him, he withdrew through hidden paths unknown to the enemy and eluded the danger. Then, a few arquebuses were aimed at the place where the corpses lay spread on the ground, and the incautious soldiers who saw to the burial of them were shot.
> >
> > Between the Horst Gate and the Gate of St. Maurice, there was in the open ground behind the walls a very tall nut-tree with thick limbs covered in foliage that hung down everywhere, and on its stronger branches a blind [hide] was built from which very many soldiers were shot and killed. For some time, the soldiers did not notice this ruse since the thickness of the branches and the foliage prevented the gun smoke from blowing away immediately. Eventually, however, people discovered the trick by peering carefully, and with large arquebuses the sharpshooter, John Nochle, was knocked down lame along with his blind, and he never appeared again.[18]

Given the relative ease with which people were able to enter and leave the city at this point in the siege, emissaries such as the surgeon Meester Gerrit van Campen, were able to reach The Netherlands where they began to urge support for Münster's cause. The authorities there grew wary when people were seen selling their property, as if preparing for a journey. The Council in Den Haag soon had possession of a circular letter for Anabaptists to assemble at the Berchklooster in Overijssel at noon on 24 March, for a trek to Münster.

Thirty ships were reported to have sailed from Monnikendam in North Holland on 21 March with twenty-seven ships held on arrival at Genemuiden in Overijssel. Five other ships were prevented from leaving Haarlem, and six were similarly detained in Amsterdam. A contemporary

---

17   3 times the length of a standard arquebus – probably requiring a rest.
18   Hermann von Kerssenbroch, (Christopher S. Mackay tr.), *Narratio Historica Anabaptistici Furoris Monasterium*, (*Narrative of the Anabaptist Madness. The overthrow of Münster, the Famous Metropolis of Westphalia*) (Leiden–Boston: Brill 2007), pp.565–566.

(although probably exaggerated) estimate that 3,000 persons were on the ships at Genemuiden was high enough for the authorities to punish only the key "leaders and baptisers", releasing the rest.[19] Despite the failed attempt, news of significant support in The Netherlands for the cause would have been heartening for the defenders and most certainly fostered the belief that at some point a relief army would be mobilised to come to their aid, a point to which I will return.

The most significant foray was that made in early April by the self-proclaimed Anabaptist prophet and leader of the rebellion – Jan Matthijs. Gresbeck related how on the eve of his excursion he had received a vision that victory was at hand,[20] resulting in a delusional sortie which he undertook with a handful of mounted men from the Ludger Gate on the following day. As many of his followers watched from the ramparts, the Bishop's horsemen converged on the small column. In vain he sought to defend himself with his double headed axe but bereft of any protection (a number of his men had already turned tail) he was soon surrounded and, stabbed with a pike, fell to the ground. Unaware of the identity of their victim, his assailants butchered him in full view of his followers:

> The landsknechts cut off his head, chopped the body into a hundred pieces and hit each other with them. They stuck the head in the air on a pole.[21]

5.3. Jan van Leiden was the illegitimate son of a Dutch mayor, and a tailor's apprentice by trade. He was born in the Dutch province of South Holland, probably in Leiden. Raised in poverty, van Leiden became a charismatic leader following the demise of Jan Mathys before the gates of the city at Easter 1534. As leader during the siege, he assumed Matthys' position as the prophet and eventually established a Royal Order complete with a Royal Court and a kingly regalia, as illustrated here. He continually had to make promises to his starving subjects about salvation from the siege and find ways of rewarding them for their enduring loyalty. This, along with his charisma, and a reign of terror, kept his position in the city secure until his eventual betrayal. His motto was *Gottesmacht is Myncracht* (God's might is my strength). (Engraving by Heinrich Aldegrever, courtesy: Rijksmuseum, Amsterdam)

---

19   James D Tracy. *Holland under Habsburg Rule 1506-1566 The Formation of a Body Politic*, (Berkeley: University of California Press 2018), p.163.
20   Heinrich Gresbeck (Christopher S. Mackay trans. and added commentary), *False Prophets and Preachers: Henry Gresbeck's Account of the Anabaptist Kingdom of Münster* (Kirksville: Truman State University Press 2016), p.89.
21   Heinrich Gresbeck (Christopher S. Mackay trans. and added commentary), *False Prophets and Preachers: Henry Gresbeck's Account of the Anabaptist Kingdom of Münster* (Kirksville: Truman State University Press 2016), p.90.

THE DEFENCE OF THE CITY 1534

The death of Mathijs was a major psychological blow to the Dutch Anabaptists who had flocked to the city. The vacuum in spiritual leadership was however swiftly taken over by a fellow Dutchman by the name of John Bockelson, the tailor otherwise known as Jan van Leiden. It would not be long before van Leiden's charisma was enabling him to reorganise the defence of the city. For a tailor and erstwhile performer, van Leiden was astute in his task ensuring that his flock maintained a strict discipline in both defence and attack. This he achieved politically by replacing the council with a committee of twelve elders with himself at its head. A new draconian defensive ordinance was drawn up (see Appendix II) ensuring that every able-bodied person was assigned a defensive task.

To arm themselves against the sovereign Prince-Bishop Franz von Waldeck and his siege, the Anabaptists began to destroy parts of the city's church steeples to make room for their artillery. As sections of the city walls were destroyed by the Bishop's siege guns during the day, the womenfolk were charged with repairing them during the night under the supervision of the city's stonemasons. This way those men manning the defences would not be fatigued should an assault be mounted.[22] Those cannonballs which landed after hitting masonry were collected and piled up in the cathedral square for reuse where possible.[23] Some women were tasked with cooking lime in copper cauldrons on the ramparts, ready to pour down onto any attackers. Others piled up rocks to be rolled down the rampart onto the enemy below.

5.4. Cannonball from the siege embedded in a part of the old city wall. (Photo courtesy: Henning Stoffers)

---

22   Hermann von Kerssenbroch, (Christopher S. Mackay tr.), *Narratio Historica Anabaptistici Furoris Monasterium*, (*Narrative of the Anabaptist Madness. The overthrow of Münster, the Famous Metropolis of Westphalia*) (Leiden–Boston: Brill 2007), p.575.
23   *Heinrich Gresbeck* (Christopher S. Mackay trans. and added commentary), *False Prophets and Preachers: Henry Gresbeck's Account of the Anabaptist Kingdom of Münster* (Kirksville: Truman State University Press 2016), p.103.

'A MIGHTY FORTRESS OF GOD': THE SIEGE OF MÜNSTER 1534-35

> ### Fouling the trenches
>
> The defenders undertook an act of villainy and wished to cover the landsknechts trenches in shit and .... placed a wine barrel in a wagon and filled it from a privy, wishing to take it to the trenches .... they gathered .... and by St. Maurice's Gate rode out of the city with the wine barrel in the direction of the trenches. When they reached the trenches with the wagon they smashed the barrel apart, and the filth ran along the trenches. Having befouled the landsknechts' trench in this way, they returned to the city.[24]

Advanced warning of any assault was crucial and thanks to defections from the Bishop's mercenaries and to captured landsknechts willing to betray their paymaster, the Anabaptists were alerted to the first assault planned for Whitsun and could be proactive. A raid to spike the Bishop's guns was planned; a detachment of men needed to be prepared for the action and the preacher Bernd Rothman[25] was called upon to rally the men with a rousing sermon.[26] The outcome of this raid was reported to the Herzog von Cleves by his war councillors in a letter dated 16 May.

> This evening at about 4 o'clock several citizens of the town attacked our siege-works. There was a skirmish, and 13 of our field guns were spiked, in addition a heavy siege cannon – the property of the city of Cologne. Several wagon wheels were smashed, and 2 tons of gunpowder ruined. According to his Grace's artillery master there are some 30 dead on both sides but mainly those from the city who did the damage. However, our commanders say that they want to have the artillery back in working order as soon as possible, so that nothing can prevent our planned bombardment and assault as outlined in our letter.[27]

---

24 Heinrich Gresbeck (Christopher S. Mackay trans. and added commentary), *False Prophets and Preachers: Henry Gresbeck's Account of the Anabaptist Kingdom of Münster* (Kirksville: Truman State University Press 2016), p.100.
25 Gresbeck nicknamed Rothmann 'Stutenberent'.
26 Heinrich Gresbeck (Christopher S. Mackay trans. and added commentary), *False Prophets and Preachers: Henry Gresbeck's Account of the Anabaptist Kingdom of Münster* (Kirksville: Truman State University Press 2016), p.104.
27 Report of the War Councillors of Herzog von Cleves to the Herzog about the Anabaptist sorties in May in Richard van Dülmen, *Das Täuferreich zu Münster 1534-1535: Berichte und Dokumente* (Munich Deutscher Taschenbuch Verlag, 1974), p.128. (Author's translation)

Plate A. Everard Alerdinck's Map of Münster.
See Colour Plate Commentaries for further information.

Plate B. Jan van Leiden, and Gatekeeper
(Illustration by Giorgio Albertini © Helion & Company)
See Colour Plate Commentaries for further information.

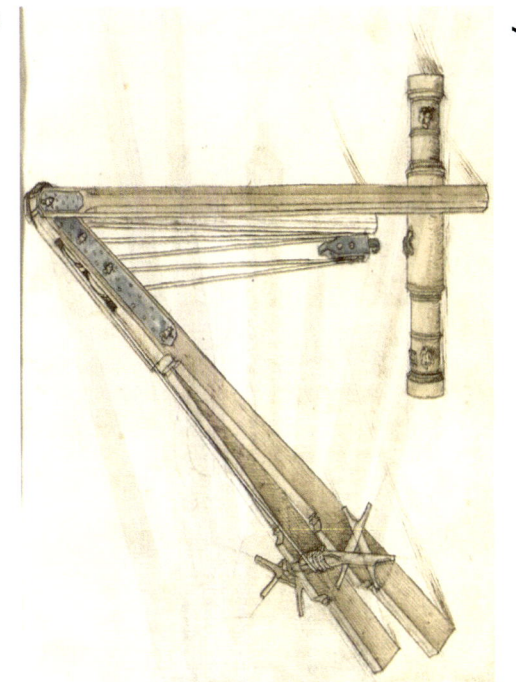
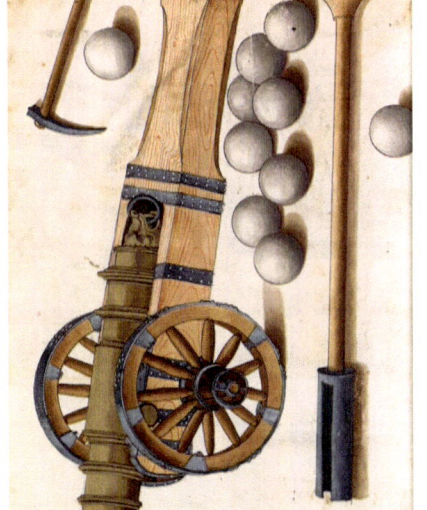

Plate C. Artillery
1. Heavy artillery piece; **2.** Siege Cannon.; **3.** Mortar; **4.** Siege cannon hoist
See Colour Plate Commentaries for further information.

iii

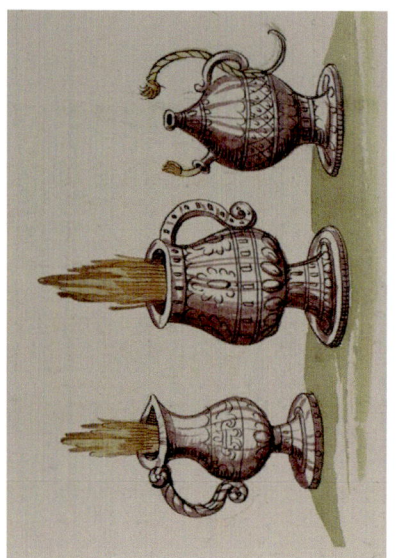

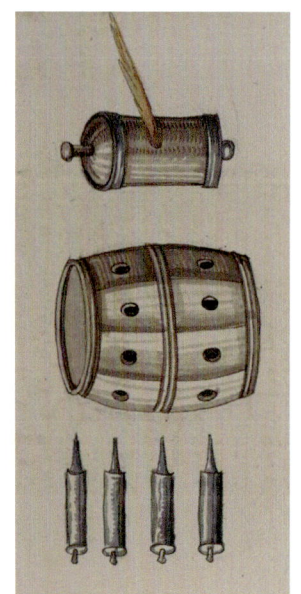
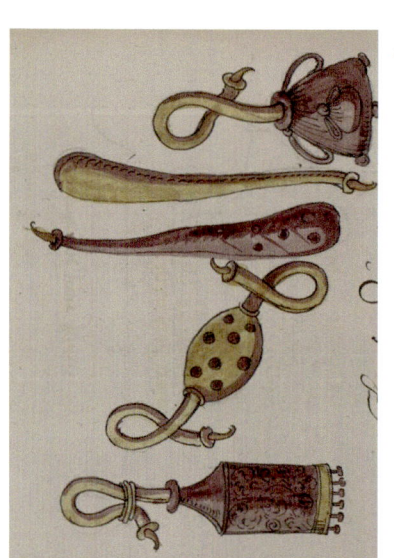
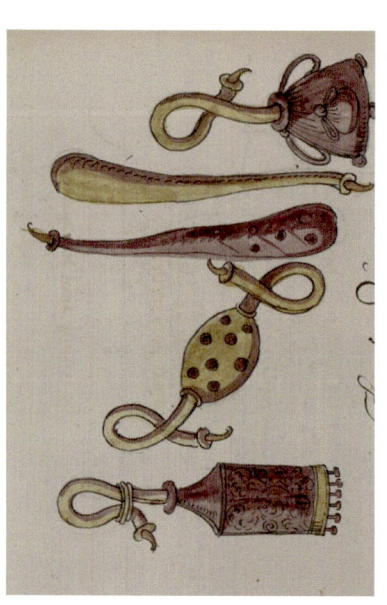

Exploding Devices from Franz Helm's *Buch der probierten Künsten*

Plate D. Explosive Devices

1. exploding barrel with metal inserts, f.61r.
2. grenades containing barbs and iron spikes, f.95v.
3. exploding wheels, f.87r.
4. early forms of Molotov cocktails containing gunpowder, f.47r.
5. exploding tree stumps, f.91v.
6. Improvised incendiary devices using pitchers, f.100r.
7. Arrow with incendiary device wrapped in a bag, f.90v.

See *Colour Plate Commentaries* for further information.

Plate E. Handgunner, cavalryman, and female defender
1. Anabaptist handgunner, April 1535
2. Member of the King's horse troop
3. Female defender

(Illustration by Giorgio Albertini © Helion & Company)
See Colour Plate Commentaries for further information.

1

2

3

4

5

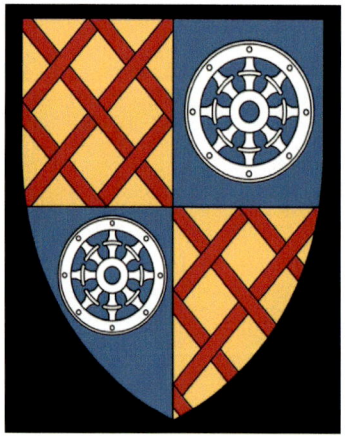

6

Plate F. Banners
1. Banner of Cologne; 2. Banner of Cleves; 3. Banner of the city of Meissen; 4. Coat of Arms of von Waldeck;
5. Heraldic sign of the Steding family; 6. Coat of Arms of Graf Wirich von Dhaun
See Colour Plate Commentaries for further information.

Plate G. Landsknecht Archer, Sapper, Standard Bearer
1. Landsknecht Archer
2. Sapper
3. Ensign Guelders Contingent
(Illustration by Giorgio Albertini © Helion & Company)
See Colour Plate Commentaries for further information.

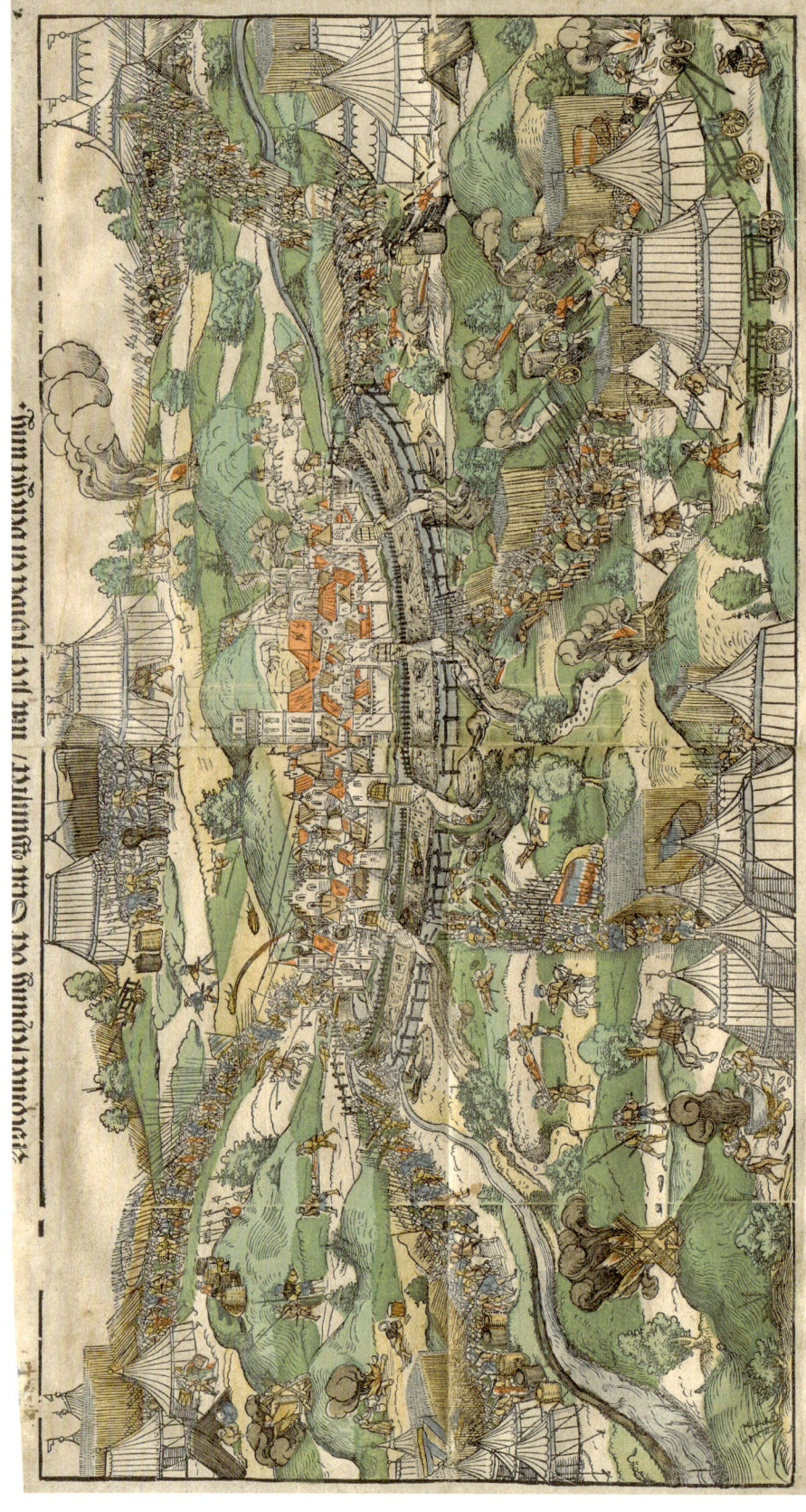

Plate H. The Siege

See Colour Plate Commentaries for further information.

THE DEFENCE OF THE CITY 1534

5.5. 'They [the defenders] made a bishop out of some hose and a shirt, and they filled it with straw and made a head on top. They hung an amice around the mannequin and put a mitre on its head and then tied the mannequin to a horse. They decked the horse out with parchments, [according to Kerssenbroch these were Papal bulls and indulgences] and brought it to the city gate. They then released it into the trenches, driving it away from themselves with a slap. The horse wth the made-up bishop ran towards the camp along the trenches. The landsknechts ran out of the camp and ran after the horse along the trenches, wanting to catch it and the man riding on it because they imagined that a live man was seated on it. When they came up to the horse, the man on it turned out to be a mannequin made of hose and a shirt stuffed with straw, the landsknechts got angry and chopped the horse and the mannequin into pieces.'[28] (illustration from Joseph Sattler, *Die Wiedertäufer* (Berlin: Verlag J. A. Stargardt, 1895)

When in August a second full assault was announced following the breakdown of negotiations, the Anabaptist defenders were thus well prepared. Jan van Leiden personally rode along the open areas behind the city walls to arrange everything necessary for the defence, ordering a company to be stationed in the cathedral square ready to be deployed to any flashpoint.

---

28   Heinrich Gresbeck (Christopher S. Mackay trans. and added commentary), *False Prophets and Preachers: Henry Gresbeck's Account of the Anabaptist Kingdom of Münster* (Kirksville: Truman State University Press 2016), pp.100–101.

'A MIGHTY FORTRESS OF GOD': THE SIEGE OF MÜNSTER 1534-35

5.6. When the assault finally came the attack was repulsed with a mix of great conviction, guile and tenacity depicted in this illustration by Joseph Sattler.[29] Kerssenbroch described the repulse of the assault in some detail:

The most appalling form of death was dealt out by the women. Some of them poured blazing lime out of wooden containers onto the enemy as they approached the fortifications. Some set fire to crowns of pitch by applying torches, and when these crowns were burning, they threw them with iron forks onto the necks of ascending soldiers. When the terrible flames penetrated their armour, these soldiers were tortured appallingly, and as they raced up and down, they fanned the flames with their increased motion. They vainly attempted to remove the burning wreaths with mitts made specifically for this purpose out of thick animal skins, but they got so stuck in the viscous blazing resin and pitch that they could not remove their hands. In the end, some fell face down onto the ground, and from the unbearable agony they rolled themselves over on the cold earth, so that the plants all around withered from the flames. Then, they spewed up their souls with a great shout. Others dived headlong into the ditches to put out the flames and sank under the weight of their armour.[30]

The successful rebuff of the Bishop's second assault on 28 August was the result of fierce defensive action on the part of the Anabaptists, graphically described by Kerssenbroch:

The townsmen not only held the onslaught of the brave soldiers but shot to death a large number of them who were either held

---

29 Joseph Sattler, *Die Wiedertäufer* (Berlin: Verlag J.A. Stargardt, 1895).
30 Hermann von Kerssenbroch, (Christopher S. Mackay tr.), *Narratio Historica Anabaptistici Furoris Monasterium*, (*Narrative of the Anabaptist Madness. The overthrow of Münster, the Famous Metropolis of Westphalia*) (Leiden–Boston: Brill 2007), p.678.

up by the fortifications or ensnared on the bramble bushes on the ramparts. Some threw down the hooked ladders and the soldiers who clung to them, killing them with a terrible fall to the ground, while others cut off the hands of soldiers holding onto the walls. Some released boards that were hung in place on top of the rampart by cutting the ropes, and with their precipitous swing downwards the boards removed the soldiers standing on the rampart and cast them down into the ditches, while others used such force in striking the ascending soldiers on their heads, which were vainly protected by helmets, that the soldiers' brains were spilled out, and with a great shout they gave up the ghost. Some used spears [pikes] to shove down the ascending soldiers, while others cut them apart with axes.

The Use of Propaganda

Van Leiden used all available means to undermine the siege. At some point, probably in June, he penned the following letter for distribution to the landsknechts either to demoralise and dissuade them from their actions and/or to persuade them to defect:

> Consider this deeply with a benevolent mind and come to us here to be enlightened through the Spirit and grace of God and to attain true recognition of the Word! You dream of nothing but the word 'money', and in your many shouts in the camps you repeat nothing but this word 'money'. Among us, however, more lofty rewards await you, and the Word of God, which you shamefully ignore, will be your pay. Put down your habits which are contrary to a Christian way of life, and shun drunkenness, fornicating, idolatry and blasphemy against God! You often send us good men who inform us about your character and way of life and what you have in mind. Why don't you enter into this way of life? Our city gates are open to those who love God. For our enemies, on the other hand, we have prepared a dish out of lime and pitch, and during the assault we will feed it to them, filling their mouths till they can eat no more. Against your *Devil* and *His Mother*, against the *Whore of Babylon*, against the *Flying Spirit*, against the *Snake of Zwolle*,[31] against mortars, falconets and other guns of this kind we will avail ourselves of the protection of the Highest One...

It had the desired effect on the men of the Meissen company under the command of Albert von Beltz encamped at the Tilgen's Gate who mutinied late in June.[32] (cf Box 4.1)

---

31 The names of some of the Bishop's siege guns.
32 Hermann von Kerssenbroch, (Christopher S. Mackay tr.), *Narratio Historica Anabaptistici Furoris Monasterium*, (Narrative of the Anabaptist Madness. The overthrow of Münster, the Famous Metropolis of Westphalia) (Leiden–Boston: Brill 2007), p.574.

Some threw stones from afar to ward off those who were rushing up, while others who were lurking in reed blinds and other forms of cover, shot soldiers from the side as they were either crossing the ditches or clinging to the ramparts.[33]

With a handful of casualties as against hundreds of the Bishop's landsknechts, the defenders would have been euphoric but chose not to launch a counterattack, so the second repulse failed to significantly influence the course of the siege in favour of the defenders.

Nevertheless, Jan van Leiden's standing as commander had been enhanced enormously. The success bolstered the conviction that the second coming of Christ was at hand and there was an increase in religious fervour with one individual in particular – a lame goldsmith by the name of Johann Dusentschur, who claimed to be a prophet. Within a few days he had proclaimed to the citizens that God had revealed to him that Jan van Leiden should be King over, 'New Israel and the whole world and would be next to God.'[34] Despite scepticism amongst the populace, Leiden's elevation was endorsed by the city leadership and in a matter of days he had abolished the council of the twelve elders and set up his royal court, with Knipperdolling as his viceroy, Rothmann as his orator, and Hermann Tilbeck as his chancellor. Kort Kruse was appointed as his commander in chief and a new defensive ordinance was drawn up in which key individuals were assigned specific military offices (see Appendix III).[35]

The smashed gates and defences were quickly rebuilt, and a huge earthwork placed before each gate. One of the 'King's' first moves was to create his own company of horse which consisted of a squadron of lancers and a detachment of mounted handgunners which carried out drills – sometimes against each other – on the cathedral square.[36] While the King basked in his new elevated position, commissioning new regalia for himself and livery for his entourage (see Plate 2), thought had to be given to the position the city now found itself in.

It was clear from information reaching him from outside that there was support for the Anabaptist cause in the countryside and further afield in

---

33   Hermann von Kerssenbroch, (Christopher S. Mackay tr.), *Narratio Historica Anabaptistici Furoris Monasterium*, (*Narrative of the Anabaptist Madness. The overthrow of Münster, the Famous Metropolis of Westphalia*) (Leiden–Boston: Brill 2007), p.678.
34   *Heinrich Gresbeck* (Christopher S. Mackay trans. and added commentary), *False Prophets and Preachers: Henry Gresbeck's Account of the Anabaptist Kingdom of Münster* (Kirksville: Truman State University Press 2016), p.134
35   *Heinrich Gresbeck* (Christopher S. Mackay trans. and added commentary), *False Prophets and Preachers: Henry Gresbeck's Account of the Anabaptist Kingdom of Münster* (Kirksville: Truman State University Press 2016), p.137.
36   *Heinrich Gresbeck* (Christopher S. Mackay trans. and added commentary), *False Prophets and Preachers: Henry Gresbeck's Account of the Anabaptist Kingdom of Münster* (Kirksville: Truman State University Press 2016), p.137

THE DEFENCE OF THE CITY 1534

the Low Countries. Whilst the Dutch defenders in Münster were pinning their hopes on a relief force coming to their aid, van Leiden began to give serious thought to how that would need to be supported. He commissioned the construction of a number of war wagons:

> …the king had a wagon fort made in expectation of the arrival of the relief. They were going to march out into the field with it when the brothers arrived from Holland and Frisia …. So they fitted out the wagon fort and had artillery placed in it consisting of demi-culverins and falconets and demi-falconets and serpentines (they also had a full field culverin cast). They also installed guns on carts, just like organ pipes standing side by side, consisting of full arquebuses. These were installed on the carts so that six or eight of the arquebuses lay side by side. Whenever they fired them, they would go off at the same time. They made the wagon fort of no more than fifteen or sixteen wagons because they didn't have the wood to make a bigger one. They also placed a palisade around the wagon fort. This palisade was arranged so that it could be carried in sections. Each section could be raised into position, and they could be spread apart. These palisades had sharp iron shafts in front, and the bottom side had an iron peg, with the palisade standing up and leaning against an iron pole. If they had hauled the wagon fort into the field, they would have fixed the palisade around it.[38]

5.7. Hille Feicken was a native of Sneek, in the Dutch province of Friesland, who had joined the 'Elect' in Münster. Early in the morning of 16 June 1534, she left the city with the intention – like Judith and Holophernes (in the Apocryphal book of Judith) – of seducing and killing Bishop Franz von Waldeck. Hille was taken prisoner by the Bishop's troops, tried, tortured, and put to death. This line drawing portrait in the style of a contemporary woodcut is from Sattler's 1895 book.[37]

---

37 Joseph Sattler, *Die Wiedertäufer* (Berlin: Verlag J.A. Stargardt, 1895).
38 *Heinrich Gresbeck* (Christopher S. Mackay trans. and added commentary), *False Prophets and Preachers: Henry Gresbeck's Account of the Anabaptist Kingdom of Münster* (Kirksville: Truman State University Press 2016), pp.177–178. Gresbeck

'A MIGHTY FORTRESS OF GOD': THE SIEGE OF MÜNSTER 1534-35

This had been a known successful tactic of the Hussites in the fifteenth century[39] and would have made it difficult for the Bishop's horse to have any impact. These wagons never made it beyond the main square where they stood in readiness following completion. Although contemporary records mention the war wagons in connection with the expectation of the arrival of a relief force in the Spring of the following year, in late October van Leiden had called a general muster of every citizen in the Cathedral square at which the citizenry was made to believe that they should prepare themselves to undertake an assault on the Bishop's positions. Around 1,600 armed men, minus those on the watch, and a further 500 old men and boys and 5,000 women presented themselves.[40]

> All the people were in the cathedral square right away as if they would march out immediately. All the men and women, young and old, came up to the cathedral square, and each had prepared and fitted himself out as if they would march out, the men with their armour and their weapons, and the women (some of them) having packed in sacks and baskets everything that they wanted to take along. So up to the cathedral square came all those who could walk, the women carrying the little children that they would take along in their arms, having slung the children in kerchiefs. There also came up to the cathedral square womenfolk who'd only just taken to the childbed and had hung the babies from their necks, the babies being no more than two or three days old. Now that they were up at the cathedral square, the men went and stood in their ranks seven deep, old people and young, everyone who could bear arms. The women all went over and stood by themselves on one side in a company.[41]

At the muster, van Leiden appointed new captains, officers, and ensigns and, from the 1,600 men able bodied present, formed a main battle (*Gewalthaufen*), a 'forlorn hope' (*verlorener Haufen*) and a detachment of skirmishers. He ordered the main battle to engage in a mock fight with the forlorn hope while his cavalry charged up and down the square.

---

notes this as occurring sometime in April, but it is reasonable to assume that this task would have required some time to fulfil and also that he had called a muster in October 1534 in expectation of an assault on the bishop's positions which would have been foolhardy without such protection (p.156).

39   Cf. Alexander Querengasser, *Hussite Warfare: The Armies, Equipment, Tactics and Campaigns 1419–1437*, (Berlin: Zeughausverlag, 2019).
40   Kerssenbroch's estimate.
41   Hermann von Kerssenbroch, (Christopher S. Mackay tr.), *Narratio Historica Anabaptistici Furoris Monasterium*, (*Narrative of the Anabaptist Madness. The overthrow of Münster, the Famous Metropolis of Westphalia*) (Leiden–Boston: Brill 2007), p.700.

THE DEFENCE OF THE CITY 1534

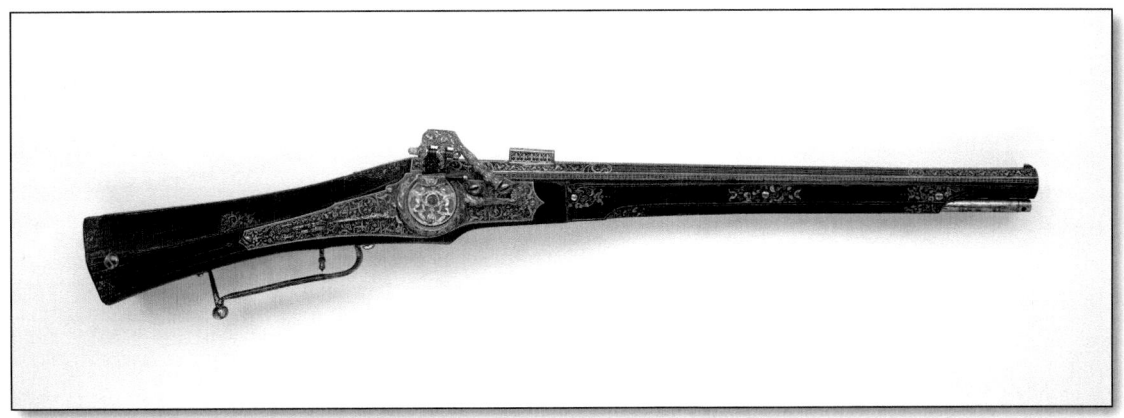

5.8. A surviving, ornate, example of a German wheelock handgun dating to 1540. The wheelock handguns that may have been carried by Jan van Leiden's mounted bodyguard, would have been less ornate than the gun shown here. Based on a friction-wheel mechanism which creates a spark that causes a firearm to fire, the wheelock was the next major development in firearms technology after the matchlock, with its name deriving from the rotating steel wheel which provided the ignition. Invented in Europe around 1500, it was superior in many ways to the cumbersome and dangerous matchlock, but its lock was a complicated mechanism and the guns were therefore expensive. It was slow, because the wheel had to be rewound after each shot before the gun could be loaded, primed, and ready to fire again. In 1517 and 1518, the first gun control laws banning the wheelock were proclaimed by the Emperor Maximilian I, initially in Austria and later throughout the Holy Roman Empire with several Italian states following suit in the 1520s and 1530s. This may account for their absence in woodcuts of the day. (Photograph courtesy of the Metropolitan Museum of Art).

This turned out to be only a drill although many of those present genuinely believed that they were about to sally forth.[42] To allay the unease caused, the King ordered a communal feast to be held in the square. At this event it was declared by Dusentschur that 27 'apostles' should be sent out to drum up support for their cause and raise a relief force. Eight men would depart by way of the Servatii Gate toward Soest; six through the Hörster Gate north toward Osnabrück; eight through the Virgin Mary's Gate west toward Coesfeld and five through the St Maurice Gate east toward Warendorf. All were to leave the city before dawn.

While the 'apostles' were able to evade the Bishop's men's watch and make for their respective targets, it was not long before most of them had been arrested, tortured and executed. However, there was one notable exception – a schoolmaster by the name of Henry Graes – who, having been apprehended by the Bishop's men, decided that treachery would be preferable to certain execution. He suggested to the Bishop that he become his agent by being dumped, in a malnourished and beaten state, in chains before one of the city's gates, whereupon he would be taken back inside and would claim that he was delivered up by an angel. Amazingly the ruse

---

42 Heinrich Gresbeck (Christopher S. Mackay trans. and added commentary), *False Prophets and Preachers: Henry Gresbeck's Account of the Anabaptist Kingdom of Münster* (Kirksville: Truman State University Press 2016), pp.160–161.

worked and Graes was allowed back into the city, becoming part of van Leiden's inner circle into the bargain.

As the year drew to a close, King Jan was determined to garner support to raise a relief army. It was important to provide a religious justification to the city's potential saviours for the stand being taken in Münster. By now the radical cleric Bernd Rothmann had fully embraced the principles of Anabaptism which he expounded in two major tracts *Restitution*,[43] published in October in the aftermath of the successful repulse of the bishop's second assault, and *Revenge*,[44] delivered in December. The latter was clearly addressed to the Melchiorites of The Netherlands. Along with three fellow travellers, Jan van Geelen, one of van Leiden's most militant Dutch supporters, was despatched to visit the cities of Deventer, Groningen, Amsterdam, Delft and Leiden, where there were Anabaptist communities, with a thousand copies of this latter tract and a substantial amount of gold. Rothmann's text laid out the religious grounds for the Kingdom of David which now prevailed in the city and as such was intended to rouse the faithful while the gold was to be used to buy weapons. The plan was to muster for a relief march on Münster which, it was hoped, would enable an assault to be made on the Bishop's positions both from the rear and by a sally from within the city itself.

Henry Graes knew that these plans were of vital importance to the Bishop and felt compelled to reveal them to the authorities. He succeeded in persuading van Leiden to allow him to become an emissary again and personally underwrite his mission to Deventer.[45] However, on leaving the city he immediately made for one of the blockhouses which had now been built, and from where he was transferred to the Bishop's palace to provide his report on what he understood to be the situation in the city at the turn of the year (see Graes's statement to the Bishop).

---

43 *Eyne Restitution edder eine Wedderstellinge rechter vnnde gesunder christliker Leer, Gelouensvnde Leuensvth Gades Genaden durch de Gemeinte Christi tho Munster an den Dach* [Tag] *gegeuenn* (1534)
44 *Eyngantztroestlich Bericht van der Wrake* [A Consoling Message of Vengeance].
45 Heinrich Gresbeck (Christopher S. Mackay trans. and added commentary), *False Prophets and Preachers: Henry Gresbeck's Account of the Anabaptist Kingdom of Münster* (Kirksville: Truman State University Press 2016), pp.168–170.

Statement given by Heinrich Graes to the Bishop, 2 January 1535

It has been decided among the leaders in Münster that they will accept eight to ten thousand fighting men, as many as they can get, and give them four gold florins a month and a free pass to engage in looting the properties of all lords and princes, both ecclesiastical and secular. This has been commanded in the Oberland, in Friesland, Holland and Wesel. They also wanted to send for a nobleman living in the country and give him fifteen thousand guilders to secretly take care of these people outside.

Six men have been sent from Münster, one to Strasbourg, called Johann van Geel, born in the monastery of Utrecht from the small village of Geel. One has gone to Friesland, a merchant born in Zütphen, whom Peter Simons brought with him from Friesland with spices and other herbs. Two Frisians have been sent to Holland and Wesel …. whose names are unknown to me. These are to foment rebellion in the aforementioned cities and countryside…

A thousand books of 3 quaterns [a 16 line poem] are to be distributed in all surrounding towns and villages, to stir up the common people so that Münster might be relieved. The book is called *Revenge*.

The food supply in Münster is almost exhausted except for three hundred cows and forty-four horses. It takes twenty cattle to provide one meal for the entire citizenry; the population is very large. There are still about thirteen hundred men and six thousand women, excluding the children. And those who wish may leave. In the space of a fortnight over two hundred have left, via St Ludger's Gate in the direction of the Agidii Gate along the Aa towards …. Mecklenbeck.

Twenty-five horses have already been eaten, cats are being roasted on a spit and mice fried in the pan. I have spoken advisably with Bernhard Rothmann, who told me: "If God does not save us from our enemies, then we shall be at our wits end; because our rye and barley is running out and will probably be gone in a month or two. However, we still have two hundred measures (*Malter*) of oats …. The king has prophesied and stated that the people of Münster would be relieved of their enemies by Easter. If this did not happen, he said, they should take him and burn him in the marketplace in front of the whole community. There are still seven tons of powder that I have seen.[46]

---

46 Richard van Dülmen, *Das Täuferreich zu Münster 1534-1535: Berichte und Dokumente* (Munich Deutscher Taschenbuch Verlag, 1974), p.215, author's translation

6

The Erection of the Blockhouses

In the camps outside the city, Bishop von Waldeck was left to pick up the pieces from the failed August assault, and a change in strategy was going to be needed. On 2 September a council of war was convened at the St Mauritz to debate the continuation of the siege. In attendance were the Princes of Cologne and of Münster, the supreme commanders of the foot and of the horse and officials of the estates. The Bishop's army had suffered around 3,000 casualties up to this point and discipline within the siege army was in tatters with troops leaving their camps in droves. After much heated debate within the council the decision was taken to convert the mercenaries' open camps into seven 'permanent' blockhouses.

Waldeck had estimated his army to be 6,000 strong but by the middle of the month he was at pains to retain half this contingent to man the planned new siegeworks. When food supplies failed to arrive, he informed his officers that if nothing arrived soon then the men were to help themselves to what they could from the outlying districts. Looting soon began in the outskirts.[1] When the Bishop's entourage left the camp at the manor of Diekburg, the mounted contingent stationed there disbanded and a part of the nobility departed with them. The council of war's proposal of 2 September to convert the mercenary camps into blockhouses was approved by the regional council at Telgte on 14 September. Of the seven original infantry camps, four that had been set up on terrain deemed too close to the city were to be moved back some distance to the designated sites of the new blockhouses. The locations of these four blockhouses are shown on the map.

---

1 Karl-Heinz Kirchhoff, 'Die Belagerung und Eroberung Münsters 1534/35' in *Westfälische Zeitschrift* volume 112 (1962), p.111.

THE ERECTION OF THE BLOCKHOUSES

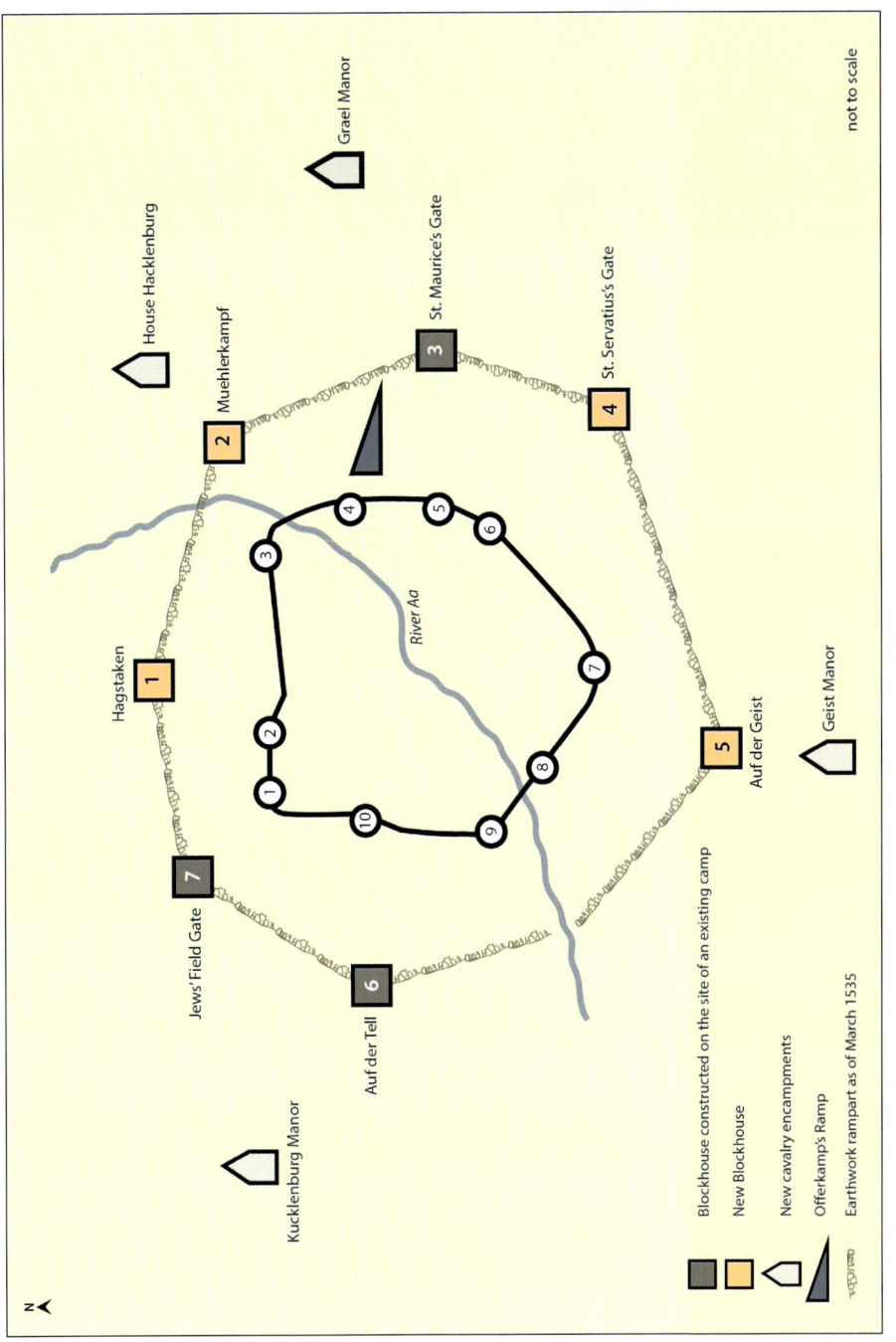

M.6. Earthworks and blockhouses from September 1534 to March 1535 based on Kirchhoff's sketches.
No.1: In front of the Cross gate, behind the former Cleves camp at the Hagstakenkam.
No.2: At the Enking mill on the adjacent Mühlenkamp, behind the former camp of Ovelacker's situated against the Hakelenburg.
No.4: In the Vale of St Servass, between the St Servatii and St Aegidii gates, in the valley on Drolshagen's meadow (Drolshagen was the owner of Haus Lütkenbeck).
No.5 Between St Aegidii and St Ludgeri Gates next to the windmill.
The remaining three blockhouses were to be constructed and encircled with a rampart and ditch at the remaining landsknecht camps (3, 6 and 7).[2]

---

2   Karl-Heinz Kirchhoff, 'Die Belagerung und Eroberung Münsters 1534/35' in *Westfälische Zeitschrift* volume 112 (1962), pp.112–113.

'A MIGHTY FORTRESS OF GOD': THE SIEGE OF MÜNSTER 1534-35

At Telgte it was also decided to set up a ring of seven camps behind the seven blockhouses for the units of horse. The existing bases at Nevinghof, Kaldenhof and Lütkenbeck were to remain while the camp at Roxel was moved to the manor at Kuddenburg. Gerd von der Recke set up a new camp at Hacklenburg manor, while Johann de Korte's horse troop established a new camp at Haus Grael. The horse of the Cathedral Chapter moved to the manor of Bischopink in the district of Geist.

Von Waldeck appointed 4 siege-work specialists to construct the blockhouses and sent word to the Archbishop that he required 2,000 labourers to carry out the work. Some 2,340 peasants from the archdiocese were to present themselves on 7 September to commence the new earthworks and a further 800 peasants from his own diocese were to commence by 14 September. Additionally, he ordered 70 lumbermen, 85 carpenters, wagons, and timber to be come to the siege. However, only a handful of peasants appeared. Following the official approval of the construction of the blockhouses on 17 September, new letters were sent to the authorities in the outlying districts to fulfil the bishop's orders.

The blockhouses were completed by the beginning of October. A survey commission described them as:

> 1. The Cleves bunker commanded by Lenz is some 125 paces square with good ramparts and a dry ditch.
> 2. The Swerhuis Blockhouse under Captain Wilhelm von Arnhem measures 125 paces square with a two-metre thick and seven-metre high rampart, surrounded by a two and a half-metre deep moat.
> 3. The Blockhouse near the ruins of the St Mauritz church is 125 paces square with a high and wide rampart and a deep and wide moat. This emplacement has four cannon and 16 hook guns.
> 4. The blockhouse in the valley commanded by Hans von Tecklenburg is 300 paces square with seven and a half-metre wide ramparts. These rise three metres high with a surrounding moat of similar depth. It is a relatively small installation equipped with two cannon and six large bore arquebuses.
> 5. The Blockhouse on the Geist commanded by Thonies Lichterte is rectangular measuring 120 x 110 paces with a five-metre thick rampart of a similar height. It is surrounded by a four metre deep by seven-metre wide ditch.
> 6. The new blockhouse under the command of Hermann Sittart has a circumference 350 paces with a three metre high rampart and a two metre deep ditch.
> 7. The Guelders Blockhouse under Egbert von Deveren measures 180 by 180 paces square and has a five foot high rampart rising out of a moat nine paces deep.[3]

---

3 Karl-Heinz Kirchhoff, 'Die Belagerung und Eroberung Münsters 1534/35' in

THE ERECTION OF THE BLOCKHOUSES

6.1. Detail of a woodcut by Hans Burgkmair depicting a blockhouse. From Marx Treitzsaurwein, *Der Weiß Kunig. Eine Erzählung von den Taten Kaiser Maximilian des Ersten, 1514-1516* (Courtesy: Universitätsbibliothek Heidelberg)

The landsknechts were to be housed in straw huts within these emplacements, but it was not long before a decision was taken to replace the straw with turf because of the risk of fire.

The blockhouse log wall was typically created by layering logs on top of each other, with the lengths of the available logs determining the size of the structure, which was usually rectangular or square in plan. The corner interlocking of the beams of the log house (see image) provided particularly good airtightness and stability. The creation of a ditch, where possible filled with water, would made any attacks from the Anabaptists that much more difficult. It can be assumed that each blockhouse would have contained slits for artillery and other firearms on all sides given the possibility of a relief

Westfälische Zeitschrift volume 112 (1962), pp.112–113.

'A MIGHTY FORTRESS OF GOD': THE SIEGE OF MÜNSTER 1534-35

6.2. Detail of blockhouse corners showing dovetail style. (Photo: Friedrich Böhringer, via Wikimedia Commons)

force coming from the rear. The expansion of the blockhouses provided some degree of relief on the bishop's war chest since it meant seven companies could be stood down with a saving of 12,000 Emden guilders per month. The nobles of the diocese were once again called upon to provide mounted contingents to patrol between the blockhouses. However, it was impossible to completely prevent the traffic of messengers, scouts, and merchants to and from the city.

In mid-October a plague broke out in the Cleves camp and the discontented mercenaries burned the camp and plundered the village of Havixbeck until they were driven out by the Bishop's horsemen. The Anabaptists took advantage of this unrest in the camp and 27 'apostles' left the city for Osnabrück, Warendorf, Soest and Coesfeld on the evening of 13 October.

The Bishop felt compelled to move with a detachment of his men against Warendorf and forced the town to surrender on 21 October.[4] Ovelacker's company remained billeted there until December 1534, with the Bishop's entourage remaining on into the New Year. At the meeting in Essen, it was decided that a commission should inspect the work undertaken on the blockhouses. This took place mid-November, and it reported that five blockhouses still required cannon and that demi-culverins should be brought from Telgte, Ahaus, Fürstenau or Warendorf. Although fifty 'double hackbuts' had been supplied, 30 still needed to be procured. Each hook gun had a powder supply for two months, plus 1,600 balls, and a further 2,000 had been ordered. Since there was a lack of horse, guard duty was not carried out at night, something which the Anabaptists would have become aware of. Following a report back in November from Theodor Fabricius, who had been sent into the city to negotiate a surrender, it was clear that the blockhouses would not suffice to entirely cut off the city. A further decision was taken to connect them by an earthwork, thereby encircling the whole of the city. This meant a bridge would have to be erected over the River Aa near the Enkingmill.

---

4   In 1533 the Anabaptist movement also spread to Warendorf and took over political control for a week in October 1534, until the short occupation was ended by Bishop Franz von Waldeck. Four Anabaptist apostles and the Warendorf Anabaptist movement leaders were beheaded in the market square. As a deterrent the bodies of the apostles were hung from the four gates into the town. As a result of this, Warendorf lost its town rights and privileges, until they were reinstated in 1542.

THE ERECTION OF THE BLOCKHOUSES

However, winter was upon the siege and completion of the ring of earthworks would have to wait.

On 11 February, the peasant sappers resumed work on the ramparts which had been postponed because of the winter conditions. A special building was also erected in the camp, in which protective mantlets and gabions could be fabricated with tough willow and reeds. The work was divided in such a way that the peasants from Wolbeck began from the right bank of the Aa flowing into the city to the blockhouse of Anton Lichtherte, then those from Bevergern and Sassenberg continued as far as the blockhouse under the command of Hans von Tecklenburg, then those of Lüdinghausen as far as the emplacement at the Castle of St Mauritz under Wilken von Steding's command. Then the peasants of Horstmar continued the work up to Willhelm von Arnhem's blockhouse, those of Dülmen and Stromberg to Lorentz von der Horst's bunker, followed by sapper contingents from Ahaus and Bocholt who built the ramparts to connect to Egbert von Deveren's blockhouse. Then the peasants of Werne toiled as far as Hermann Syttard's blockhouse and from there to the left bank of the Aa. These were relieved after 5 days by peasant sappers from Harpstedt, Wildeshausen, Vechta, Emsland, Kloppenburg and Delmenhorst. The whole of the city would eventually be surrounded by a sloping ditch and a steep rampart in which thorny bushes and poles were randomly inserted to bind the heaps of sandy soil.

6.3. Detail of simple corner combing for logs. (Photo: Giacomo via Wikimedia Commons)

The sight of the construction of the blockhouses and connecting earthworks began to have a demoralising effect on the Anabaptists. As Gresbeck wrote:

> The king (van Leiden) and all the re-baptisers imagined that my Gracious Lord of Münster [i.e. the Bishop] was going to withdraw from the city in the end. But when they began to make the blockhouses, the realm (the area of no man's land between the outer works and the siege lines) took shape in front of the city, and they wouldn't leave the city (they would capture it first) – as soon as the trench was dug all the way round the city, from one blockhouse to the next, with small block houses built in between and a high trench was edged with hawthorn, they gave the city up as lost. As soon as the trench was dug around the city no one could rush into the city or get out of it after that time. All too few were those who made it out of the city. No more than five or six made it across. After that

'A MIGHTY FORTRESS OF GOD': THE SIEGE OF MÜNSTER 1534-35

6.4. Sconce – an early form of pillbox. Woodcut by Erhard Schön from the Siege of Münster series. (LWL-Museum für Kunst und Kultur, Westfälisches Landesmuseum, Münster)

time they couldn't get any news into the city, and they also couldn't get any letter out of the city, so that then the city was lost …. the landsknechts had also manned the trench …. with a watch at night, and they kept a watch during the day on horseback and on foot, so that it was pretty much impossible for anyone to get away.[5]

---

5   Heinrich Gresbeck (Christopher S. Mackay trans. and added commentary), *False Prophets and Preachers: Henry Gresbeck's Account of the Anabaptist Kingdom of Münster* (Kirksville: Truman State University Press 2016), pp.232–223.

7

The Defence of the City 1535

Much had happened within the city since the successful defence against the bishop's siege during the previous year. There had been failed open challenges to the leadership, at times questioning the authenticity of Jan Matthijs' claim to be a prophet.[1] All property had been collectivised and a new council of elders chosen which was responsible for maintaining discipline during the siege with mayor Knipperdolling appointed as the city executioner. Following Matthijs's fatal sortie, Jan van Leiden had immediately asserted himself as the spiritual leader. All books apart from the scriptures were burned and parts of the city's churches were blown up and the rubble was to be used to bolster the fortifications and artillery positions.[2] With women outnumbering men three to one, van Leiden had taken a decision to legitimise polygamy in May which had prompted a failed uprising and given further weight to the Bishop's cause.[3]

The repulse of the Bishop's second assault in August had greatly enhanced Jan van Leiden's position and, in September, he had declared himself 'King over New Israel' and set up a new court and defensive ordinance (see Appendix III). In November, unsuccessful peace overtures had been made to the King by Landgraf Philipp von Hessen's emissary Theodor Fabricius. However, by the end of the year, as winter set in and the full blockade of the city was underway, conditions and morale in the city began to deteriorate. The leadership knew that support from abroad and from the Dutch Melchiorites

---

1   *Heinrich Gresbeck* (Christopher S. Mackay trans. and added commentary), *False Prophets and Preachers: Henry Gresbeck's Account of the Anabaptist Kingdom of Münster* (Kirksville: Truman State University Press 2016), pp.77–81.

2   Max Geisberg, erstwhile curator of the city museum began excavations at the Crossgate in 1897and unearthed evidence that the Anabaptists had reinforced the earthworks there with statues of saints and baptismal fonts from the cathedral and the Overwater church. Https://www.sto-ms.de/bildgeschichte/promenade (accessed 26 July 2023).

3   *Heinrich Gresbeck* (Christopher S. Mackay trans. and added commentary), *False Prophets and Preachers: Henry Gresbeck's Account of the Anabaptist Kingdom of Münster* (Kirksville: Truman State University Press 2016), pp.124–130.

in particular, was going to be crucial. Thanks to an inadequate manning of the earthworks surrounding the city, which had been commented on by the council of war's inspection in November, the Anabaptists had been able to send its apostles and procurers out of the city.

In January 1535 Jan stepped up his efforts to rouse support abroad. At Zandt, a village in The Netherlands province of Groningen, there had been considerable Anabaptist activity during the previous year with visits by the Munsterite emissaries Jacob Cremer and Antonius Kistemaker. In the new year a large meeting of a thousand followers was held on the De Arke Farm near the village where baptisms were undertaken and a decision was taken to raise a troop to march on Münster. However, when news of an approaching army reached them, the gathering dispersed.

Back in Münster van Leiden was pinning his hopes on a relief army but knew that as the winter closed in, he would have to maintain strict discipline within the city. On 2 January he had a new ordinance published to keep the people in the city and strengthen their resolve. In key articles:

> any attempt to stir up sedition would be punishable by death. Any quarrels in detachments manning the defences leading to mortal injury of a fellow defender would likewise incur the penalty of death for the offenders. No one could withdraw from the camps without having obtained permission and leave from his commander. Three days absence without his wife's knowledge or obtaining permission from his commander, left the wife free to seek marriage with someone else. No one was allowed to access a watch post either by day or by night unless the enemy was launching an assault, and/or he had specific instructions from a superior to make the rounds to keep close watch on the guards, or for some other necessity. Anyone violating such a rule would not escape punishment.[4]

Enforcing such provisions and maintaining the regime of polygamy with the executioner's sword (at his confession Knipperdolling claimed to have beheaded up to 12 individuals, including women who had refused to sleep with their imposed husbands) fostered an atmosphere of terror.[5] Altogether, about 80 people were executed in the city: the first open critic of the self-claimed prophets – the blacksmith Hubert Rüscher who had denounced Matthys; 15 landsknechts who had defected from the bishop's ranks; the 47 conspirators of the so-called Mollenheck uprising against the introduction of polygamy in July of the previous year; 6 women (including one of van

---

4   Hermann von Kerssenbroch, (Christopher S. Mackay tr.), *Narratio Historica Anabaptistici Furoris Monasterium*, (*Narrative of the Anabaptist Madness. The overthrow of Münster, the Famous Metropolis of Westphalia*) (Leiden–Boston: Brill 2007), pp.653– 655.

5   Richard van Dülmen, *Das Täuferreich zu Münster 1534-1535: Berichte und Dokumente* (Munich Deutscher Taschenbuch Verlag, 1974), p.271.

THE DEFENCE OF THE CITY 1535

7.1. This early fifteenth century design of a war wagon from *Medieval Housebook of the Family Waldburg/Wolfegg* by an unknown artist gives an impression of how one of the 16 wagons might have been constructed. Note how the wagon was pushed rather than drawn with the horses appearing to be barded. Any guns mounted in the wagons would have had to have been breech loading and/or constructed on a swivel to enable loading from the inside of the wagon. (Public domain)

Leiden's wives) for violation of the marriage regulations; and in the spring of 1535, a further 10 individuals for alleged treason. During the last weeks of the siege there were also further executions in Münster. Clas Nordhorn confessed under torture that he had written to the Prince-Bishop and offered to turn traitor. He was beheaded by the king, as was another man, who tried to drive the last cows, grazing before the gates, into the hands of the besiegers.[6]

Van Leiden proclaimed that the relief would come at Easter. The fantasy was that a 100,000 strong army would not only liberate the city but also take control of the bishopric and that of Osnabrück, Cologne and the territory of Cleves.[7] The war wagons which were to be used to support the relief army as it entered the siege area had now been completed and stood ready in the Cathedral Square to provide cover for the Anabaptist sortie. Rothmann's text *On Vengeance* which had been sent to The Netherlands and Frisia was urging everyone to rise, take up arms and march to the New Israel (Münster). It was claimed that correspondence from The Netherlands and Frisia, probably from van Geel, would be relayed to the citizenry as a revelation from God.[8] Van Leiden and his council began preparing for the march out of the city to meet the relief force.

---

6   Ralf Klötzer, 'The Melchiorites in Münster' in Stayer, James, Roth, John (Eds.) *A Companion to Anabaptism and Spiritualism, 1521-1700* (Leiden: Brill, 2006), p.249.
7   Heinrich Gresbeck (Christopher S. Mackay trans. and added commentary), *False Prophets and Preachers: Henry Gresbeck's Account of the Anabaptist Kingdom of Münster* (Kirksville: Truman State University Press 2016), p.183.
8   Heinrich Gresbeck (Christopher S. Mackay trans. and added commentary), *False*

'A MIGHTY FORTRESS OF GOD': THE SIEGE OF MÜNSTER 1534-35

A call to muster was issued to the true believers. All the volunteers assembled and 'equipped themselves with weaponry and armour and clothed themselves in hose and doublets, made '*à la landsknecht*'.[9] They took part in weekly drills on the Cathedral Square, often engaging in mock battles. Although many had honed their skills as snipers, picking off the bishop's men from the outer works, the vast majority had no experience of armed combat on the field of battle. Some 300 men, young and old, were to be retained to man the defences, and thought had to be given to the scenario where the majority of able-bodied men would be in the field leaving a small garrison to look after the city.[10] Similarly, a call went out to the womenfolk who outnumbered the men three to one to present themselves at a muster for the march out of the city. About 300 women appeared at the muster on the Cathedral Square with their weaponry:

> …one with a halberd, another with a handled spear[11] and in this way they formed ranks. The womenfolk who wished to take part in the march out whom the King wished to take along numbered about fifty actually and they were listed under their names.[12]

Those women who were to remain were still expected to assemble like companies of landsknechts. They were divided into ten companies with ranks three deep to cover each gate where they were assigned specific posts by each gate commander.

As Easter arrived and the relief failed to materialise, van Leiden's credibility and legitimacy was once again being put to the test. Efforts had indeed been made to raise an army, but these had foundered in a clash against a force under the command of Jorg Schenk at the Old Cloister at Bolsward in Friesland.

Pastor Rothmann was called upon to provide some rationale for the non-appearance of a relief force:

> Dear brothers and sisters …. we are relying on our foreign brothers who are supposed to come to us. This is not what we should rely on.

Prophets and Preachers: Henry Gresbeck's Account of the Anabaptist Kingdom of Münster (Kirksville: Truman State University Press 2016), p.179.

9   *Heinrich Gresbeck* (Christopher S. Mackay trans. and added commentary), *False Prophets and Preachers: Henry Gresbeck's Account of the Anabaptist Kingdom of Münster* (Kirksville: Truman State University Press 2016), p.176.

10   *Heinrich Gresbeck* (Christopher S. Mackay trans. and added commentary), *False Prophets and Preachers: Henry Gresbeck's Account of the Anabaptist Kingdom of Münster* (Kirksville: Truman State University Press 2016), p.182.

11   Probably an eel pike.

12   *Heinrich Gresbeck* (Christopher S. Mackay trans. and added commentary), *False Prophets and Preachers: Henry Gresbeck's Account of the Anabaptist Kingdom of Münster* (Kirksville: Truman State University Press 2016), p.182.

THE DEFENCE OF THE CITY 1535

7.2. Jan van Leyden sent Jan van Geel (Geelen) not only to distribute copies of Rothmann's books throughout the Netherlands, but also to conduct attacks to shift focus away from Münster. On 29 March 1535, 200 Anabaptists stormed and occupied the Old Cloister building in Bolsward, in Friesland in The Netherlands. The battle for the building represented a serious threat to the local authorities because, if it were successful, the possibility of a larger rebellion might greatly increase. A group of 70 Anabaptists from Groningen formed to assist those in the Old Cloister. After eight days of fighting, the building was recaptured and all its occupants were killed, except for Geel, who managed to escape. After Bolsward, Geel sought to build a force to take control of Amsterdam, where there was a large Anabaptist community. Presenting himself to the Habsburg authorities as an emissary sent to negotiate the surrender of Münster, he was granted safe passage and freedom of movement throughout the city. There, he covertly attempted to garner support from the Anabaptist sects, as well as Protestant sympathizers. On 10 May 1535, Geel attacked and seized the city hall of Amsterdam with a force of about 60 men. However, additional support never materialized and Geel, along with his remaining 40 followers, were all killed when the city's *schutters* retook the building on the morning of 11 May. (Courtesy of Rijksmuseum, Amsterdam)

God will certainly relieve us when it is our time. But if they come, we will take them as reinforcement.[13]

However, it was becoming clear to the diehard Anabaptists in the city that the only relief which God was going to provide would be death by starvation. Bizarrely, to maintain morale against such a backdrop, the King

---

13   *Heinrich Gresbeck* (Christopher S. Mackay trans. and added commentary), *False Prophets and Preachers: Henry Gresbeck's Account of the Anabaptist Kingdom of Münster* (Kirksville: Truman State University Press 2016), p.184.

ordered 3 days of festivities (one third of the citizenry was to come on each day) but the availability of bread as the only sustenance on the benches which were laid out could not distract increasing numbers of the defenders from thinking that their time was up.[14]

Since November, when the last grain stocks had been collected, private baking and brewing had been forbidden. Bread and beer were produced and distributed centrally. On three occasions in March the three night watch groups into which the community was divided participated in a common meal of bread and beer. At the beginning of each meal van Leiden appeared at a window of one of the houses on Cathedral Square to read from the Bible about the battles of King David and how an angel with a glowing sword had come from the heavens and driven the enemies away. Jan van Leiden amplified, 'Dear brothers, the same thing can happen to us. The same God lives.' When famine began to set in the king proclaimed, 'Anyone who still has something must share with his brother.'

On 3 May, the last reorganisation of the city's defence took place. Companies were mustered in the cathedral square and one after another, sworn in by Rothmann to give their lives for the cause in the coming battle.

7.3. Jan van Leyden as King of the Anabaptists sitting with his council and positioned between his wives. Dusentschur and Knipperdolling are represented nude, the latter with the executioner's sword. Drawing by Heinrich Aldegrever, 1535-1558. (Courtesy Rijksmuseum, Amsterdam).

---

14   *Heinrich Gresbeck* (Christopher S. Mackay trans. and added commentary), *False Prophets and Preachers: Henry Gresbeck's Account of the Anabaptist Kingdom of Münster* (Kirksville: Truman State University Press 2016), pp.185–194.

Shortly thereafter, because of the food shortage, the men were allowed to release their "lesser wives" from the city.[15]

Early in May van Leiden received a dream from God himself in which he was told to bid the people to select twelve princes to help the King govern the twelve tribes of Israel.[16] This prompted him to organise the election of twelve 'dukes' to be chosen by the citizens dwelling at each gate. This democratic practice represented a clear snub to the Bishop and nobility on the outside, but it also served a military purpose in that it created new structures of responsibility at key positions of defence within the city.[17] Each of the 10 gates now had a commanding officer with a retinue. In addition, one duke was to take up position at 'Uldan's Fort', a sconce between St Ludger's Gate and St Servatius's Gate and one at the new blockhouse by the New Bridge Gate (see Map, Chapter 2).

This initiative could not lift the defenders' morale, however. As starvation worsened, van Leiden realised that it was necessary to give special dispensation to the old and the frail and those weakened by starvation.[18] Towards the end of April permits had already been issued and a steady stream of Anabaptists had begun to leave the city. Up to June between 1,500 to 2,000 men, women, and children were expelled or otherwise encouraged to leave. Between 600 and 700 of these male refugees were killed by the Bishop's troops.[19] In amongst this number were also small groups who had found a means of escape. In one such group were two former landsknechts – Henry Gresbeck and Hans van der Langenstraat – who, with three other comrades, sought to save their skins by disclosing to the bishop's men the means by which a successful assault on the city could be carried out.

---

15   Ralf Klötzer, 'The Melchiorites in Münster' in Stayer, James, Roth, John (Eds.) *A Companion to Anabaptism and Spiritualism, 1521-1700* (Leiden: Brill, 2006), p.249.

16   MacKay, footnote in Hermann von Kerssenbroch, (Christopher S. Mackay tr.), *Narratio Historica Anabaptistici Furoris Monasterium,* (*Narrative of the Anabaptist Madness. The overthrow of Münster, the Famous Metropolis of Westphalia*) (Leiden–Boston: Brill 2007), p.773.

17   *Heinrich Gresbeck* (Christopher S. Mackay trans. and added commentary), *False Prophets and Preachers: Henry Gresbeck's Account of the Anabaptist Kingdom of Münster* (Kirksville: Truman State University Press 2016), pp.244–250.

18   Kerssenbroch gives a graphic if somewhat dramatic account of the situation in the city. Hermann von Kerssenbroch, (Christopher S. Mackay tr.), *Narratio Historica Anabaptistici Furoris Monasterium,* (*Narrative of the Anabaptist Madness. The overthrow of Münster, the Famous Metropolis of Westphalia*) (Leiden–Boston: Brill 2007), pp.673–681.

19   Willem De Bakker, Michael Driedger and James Stayer, *Bernhard Rothmann and the Reformation in Münster, 1530-35* (Kitchener: Pandora Press 2009), p.180.

8

The Final Assault

1535

11 February	Work restarts on the erection of the rampart linking the blockhouses
March	Starvation in the city begins to take effect. The old and the frail are released into the Bishop's camps
April/May	Exodus continues and includes two defectors Henry Gresbeck and Hans van der Langenstraat who suggest a plan to mount a night assault
24/25 June	Final assault Münster is retaken

Following a decision taken at the meeting of the Imperial Circle at Worms on 10 January *Graf* Wirich von *Dhaun*-Falkenstein assumed supreme field command. As early as November 1534 at the assembly at Essen, the Koblenz representative had proposed the construction of a circumvallation between the blockhouses to prevent any movement into and out of the city. Wirich von Dhaun was committed to seeing these earthworks completed. They were to comprise seven sections between the blockhouses and consist of a rampart and ditch reinforced with thickets and palisades. After the weather had prevented work in January 1535, with the ditches being full of water, it was not until 12 February that Graf Dhaun could report the start of any digging. All the estates to the north and south of the bishopric were instructed in February to send a total of 3,000 men. At first, only a handful of peasants turned up, the estates having other use for their subjects. Thus, by March little progress had been made and matters were made more urgent as prisoners and defectors from the city reported that the Anabaptists were expecting a relief army from the Netherlands at Easter (28 March) and that there were plans to break through the siege ring with a train of 'war wagons'.[1]

Dhaun warned the Bishop that the earthworks would remain unfinished, and the gates at the blockhouses would lie open, since no workers had come. He pleaded with the Bishop to ensure that the work would continue day and night. By April 1535, the last gaps in the earthworks had been filled. Access from outside was now impossible. However, any direct assault on the city had been abandoned.[2] The plan was to starve the city into submission. Those cities and nobles which had loaned siege artillery to the Bishop a year earlier were thus now demanding their return.

The full blockade plan however soon began to work. On 10 April Graf Dhaun reported to the Bishop that old people, women, and children were fleeing in droves from the city and were remaining in front of the entrenchments. They were a pitiable sight and clearly chose to be at the mercy of the Bishop rather than starve to death. There was no appetite to punish such wretched beings but at the same time the besiegers did not want to run the risk of these refugees spreading discord throughout the region. Consensus within the Bishop's inner circle was that they should be sent back into the city. However, the Bishop eschewed such an approach. Short of complete surrender he suggested that, as a deterrent, a refugee city dweller be executed, placed on a stake and wheel outside a city gate, and a note attached to the post with the warning: 'This is what happens to all those who come out of the city.' On 26 April, four refugees were indeed taken prisoner, beheaded, and their bodies placed on a stake and wheel before the gates.[3]

Citizens continued to leave the city. By 7 May, about 200 to 300 refugees were gathering in the no man's land between the outer works and the new rampart. By 3 June, the number had swelled to around 400 men, 400 women and a great number of children. Every day up to 50 men were put to death by the bishop's landsknechts. Even those fellow mercenaries in the pay of the city who had left were given no quarter. The female sutlers, camp prostitutes and other women in the blockhouses took pity on the women and children who remained lying in no-man's land and supplied them with bread. Later the children were taken into the blockhouses.[4]

---

1 Karl-Heinz Kirchhoff, 'Die Belagerung und Eroberung Münsters 1534/35' in *Westfälische Zeitschrift* volume 112 (1962), p.133.
2 As late as June, Justinius von Holzhausen was informing his father that he couldn't see the city being taken that summer without some act of treachery on behalf of the defendants. Letter dated 8 June in Carl Adolf Cornelius, *Berichte der Augenzeugen uber das Münsterische Wiedertäuferreich* (London: Forgotten Books 2018 reprint), pp.355–356.
3 Hermann von Kerssenbroch, (Christopher S. Mackay tr.), *Narratio Historica Anabaptistici Furoris Monasterium*, (*Narrative of the Anabaptist Madness. The overthrow of Münster, the Famous Metropolis of Westphalia*) (Leiden–Boston: Brill 2007), p.137.
4 Hermann von Kerssenbroch, (Christopher S. Mackay tr.), *Narratio Historica*

'A MIGHTY FORTRESS OF GOD': THE SIEGE OF MÜNSTER 1534-35

The refugee situation was becoming critical by the day and Count Dhaun and his council of war could not come to a decision in this matter. The Bishop was ill and not present in the camp, so the issue was tabled for decision at the Diet held in Dülmen on 19 May. The estates agreed that they did not want to have anything to do with the refugees, and that they should hand the men over to the supreme commander who would deal with the matter accordingly, while the women should be taken to the manor of Diekburg where a decision could be made about their fate. Natives of the environs of Münster were to remain in their homes under supervision until the end of the war while foreigners were to be returned to their home countries. Philipp von Hessen, who did not want to be party to any decision resulting in capital punishment involving women, preferred that they be instructed to swear a new oath of allegiance and be sent on their way while those men who had willingly joined the sect be judged accordingly. The council of war's members wanted to leave the responsibility for the fugitives to the Bishop and complained that they were being made judges and executioners of the women.

On 23 May a small number of defectors had made their way through one of the secret passageways and out into the open. In amongst this group of five men were two former landsknechts by the name of Henry Gresbeck and Hans van der Langenstraat. Langenstraat had deserted from the bishop's army in 1534 and defected to the city, even becoming one of the royal men-at-arms. As *persona non grata* in the camps he therefore sought initial protection from his former commanding officer, Meinhard von Hamm. Gresbeck on the other hand had no previous cause to incur the wrath of the Bishop's mercenaries and made the risky trek across no-man's land to the Guelders blockhouse opposite the Jews' Field Gate. Both, acting out of self-preservation, were keen to surrender, insisting that they had information to share with the siege commanders as to the best way to penetrate the city in a night assault. Darkness had proven to be a crucial time during a siege. It was not only the time of secrecy, betrayal, and invisibility, it was the time during which activity during sieges was at its most intense. This is when moats could be diverted, attack positions built, defences repaired, and supplies secured for a besieged fortress.[5]

It took almost a month before this new information could be checked out and a decision taken to prepare for a night assault.[6] Having failed twice

---

Anabaptistici Furoris Monasterium, (Narrative of the Anabaptist Madness. The overthrow of Münster, the Famous Metropolis of Westphalia) (Leiden–Boston: Brill 2007), p.678.

5   Sven Petersen, 'Achim Landwehr, Im "Schleier der Nacht": Dunkelheit und Unsichtbarkeit als Faktoren frühneuzeitlicher Belagerungen in Arbeitskreis Militär und Gesellschaft in der Frühen Neuzeit' e.V. 2017 *Militär und Zeit in der Frühen Neuzeit, Vol 21.* (Potsdam: Universität Verlag, 2017)

6   *Heinrich Gresbeck* (Christopher S. Mackay trans. and added commentary), *False Prophets and Preachers: Henry Gresbeck's Account of the Anabaptist Kingdom of Münster* (Kirksville: Truman State University Press 2016), pp.266–271.

THE FINAL ASSAULT

before, the siege commanders were highly apprehensive insisting on several inspections of the location for the proposed night attack before any such raid could be launched:

> So Little Hans (Langenstraat) and the burgher (Gresbeck) went back to the city one more time with a captain, Lenz von Horst, and other officers as the burgher had done once before. They inspected the city once again including the moat and the wall, to see if everything there was still in the state that it had been before. The burgher climbed into the canal and measured the canal with a pike to see how wide it was, with Little Hans. They didn't find any of the rebaptisers holding watch up on the wall, with everything still as it had been. They moved back from there to the (Guelders) blockhouse…[7]

While eight wagons full of ladders and two gangways were brought up to the blockhouse, the Bishop was obliged to negotiate with his landsknechts over the question of booty. Their willingness to follow orders could not be guaranteed unless an accommodation could be made on this issue. Anxious to avoid a repeat of the debacle of the first assault, orders were given for the sutlers to refrain from dispensing wine or beer to the men in the hours prior to the assault. At 11p.m. on 14 June, Gresbeck and Langenstraat set out from the Cleves blockhouse opposite the Cross Gate followed by groups of peasants carrying the ladders and gangways. It was by all accounts a miserable night and the incessant rain had caused the city defenders to retreat into their bunkers on the outer works at the Cross Gate.[8]

Approaching the outer moat, Gresbeck and an assistant tethered ropes to the gangway, tied the same around their waists and let themselves down the ditch into the moat. Swimming across, they pulled the gangway across behind them and reaching the foot of the rampart climbed up and fastened it to the palisade at the top with iron hooks.[9] They then ushered van

---

7   Heinrich Gresbeck (Christopher S. Mackay trans. and added commentary), *False Prophets and Preachers: Henry Gresbeck's Account of the Anabaptist Kingdom of Münster* (Kirksville: Truman State University Press 2016), p.271.
8   Heinrich Gresbeck (Christopher S. Mackay trans. and added commentary), *False Prophets and Preachers: Henry Gresbeck's Account of the Anabaptist Kingdom of Münster* (Kirksville: Truman State University Press 2016), p.271.
9   Kerssenbroch gives a different account of the crossing
    Here the ditches were narrow and low in water, and beside the aged wooden beam with teeth that held up the wickerwork across the surface of the water to ward off the enemy, the soldiers threw into these ditches bundles of straw and shrubbery each soldier had brought a bundle with him from the camps tree stumps and branches, ladders, wood, clumps of turf, cheaper wagons with twigs, and whatever chance offered. With the help of this hurriedly built bridge, they broke the wickerwork and crossed the first ditch.
    Hermann von Kerssenbroch, (Christopher S. Mackay tr.), *Narratio Historica*

'A MIGHTY FORTRESS OF GOD': THE SIEGE OF MÜNSTER 1534-35

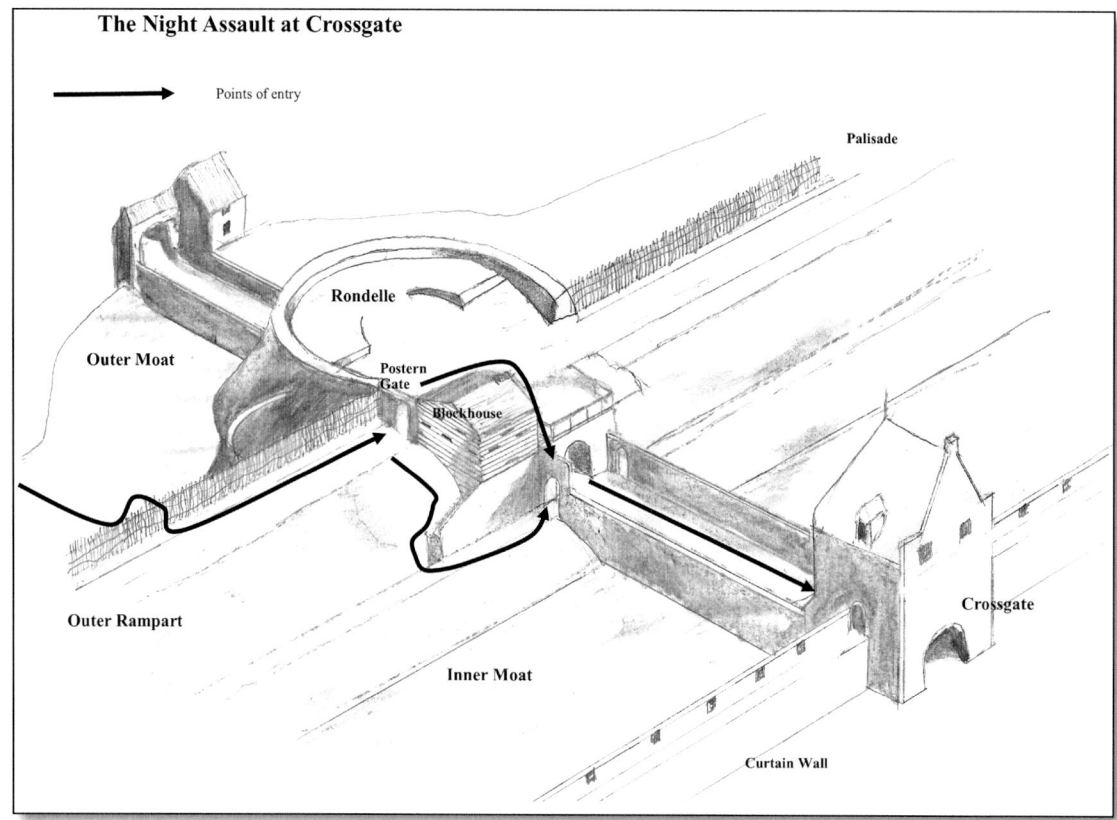

8.1. The night incursion at the Cross Gate. Sketch by the author based on a detailed drawing by Max Geisberg, former curator of the city museum.

Langenstraat across to test the gangway and bring ladders across to fix to the palisade so that an initial group of 35 landsknechts under the command of Wilken Steding could cross the rampart and climb over the palisade. In the main company were the officers Egbert von Deveren, Herman Sittard, Louis von Brunswick and Lawrence von Horst. Johann von Twickel was appointed ensign. While Gresbeck stood in the moat steadying the gangway, Langenstraat led the men up to the watch at the gate.

> Virtually at its summit were placed sharp-pointed stakes that were arranged in a row at moderate intervals so that they would throw back or at least slow down anyone ascending. Since this rampart was steep, they mounted it by climbing at an angle, but when they reached the stakes that stuck up at the top, Little Hans removed one of them which he had noted earlier, so that those ascending could

---

Anabaptistici Furoris Monasterium, (*Narrative of the Anabaptist Madness. The overthrow of Münster, the Famous Metropolis of Westphalia*) (Leiden–Boston: Brill 2007), pp.692–693.

Given Gresbeck's personal involvement in the action this account appears unlikely for the Cross gate but may well have described the situation at the Jews' Field Gate, the crossing point of the main force in the early hours of 25 June.

climb up to the top of the bulwark without much difficulty.[10]

Beckoning the next squad over to launch the attack, a further 50 men began to cross the gangway, but it gave way throwing them into the moat and causing Gresbeck to once again swim across to reinstate it. Within a short space of time about 400 men had crossed the moat and had made their way through a small postern gate which provided access for the watch to the palisade on the outer rampart. Armed with their short swords (*katzbalger*), this advanced troop overpowered and silenced the watch along this section of the outer works and made their way through the gatehouse into the city. The plan seems to have been twofold. Firstly, to secure both the gatehouse to provide access for Graf Dhaun and the main force which was assembling quietly at the Guelders blockhouse between the Cross and Jews' Field Gates and secondly, to push through to the cathedral to neutralise the Anabaptist's main arsenal there. Although Langenstraat had argued that the city could be taken with 400 men (intelligence had estimated the number of armed defenders at 800 with perhaps only 200 properly fed and watered), the alarm was raised, and a squad of defenders rushed to the sconce on the roundel (see image) and attacked the tail end of the vanguard charged with securing the Cross Gate. Here the Anabaptist defenders proved successful in driving the Bishop's men into the streets and closing the postern gate making it impossible for any backdoor incursion and more importantly preventing the opening of the outer Cross Gate. Given the heavy casualties incurred during the failed second assault at the gatehouses, there would have been apprehension on the part of the Bishop's commanders in the absence of any assurances that the gate had been taken. Since Wilken von Steding's vanguard was now in the city, they had been effectively cut off. Their fellow mercenaries waiting to enter believed that this had been all been part of an Anabaptist ruse on the part of Langenstraat and Gresbeck to trap the advanced party in the city and massacre them. Others thought that the vanguard had purposefully closed the gate to maximise their share of the booty.[11]

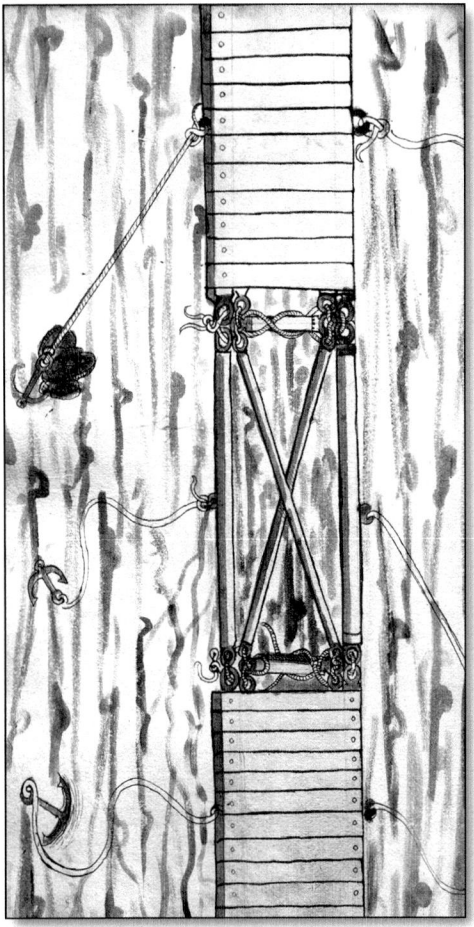

8.2. Portable footbridge. Drawing from the Kriegs- u. Feuerwerkbuch des Ludwig Eyb vom Hartenstein, Franken 1500; (Ms H2/MS.B 26, 162r. Courtesy: Universitätsbibliothek Erlangen)

---

10   Hermann von Kerssenbroch, (Christopher S. Mackay tr.), *Narratio Historica Anabaptistici Furoris Monasterium*, (*Narrative of the Anabaptist Madness. The overthrow of Münster, the Famous Metropolis of Westphalia*) (Leiden–Boston: Brill 2007), p.693. This description certainly seems plausible.
11   cf *Heinrich Gresbeck* (Christopher S. Mackay trans. and added commentary), *False*

'A MIGHTY FORTRESS OF GOD': THE SIEGE OF MÜNSTER 1534-35

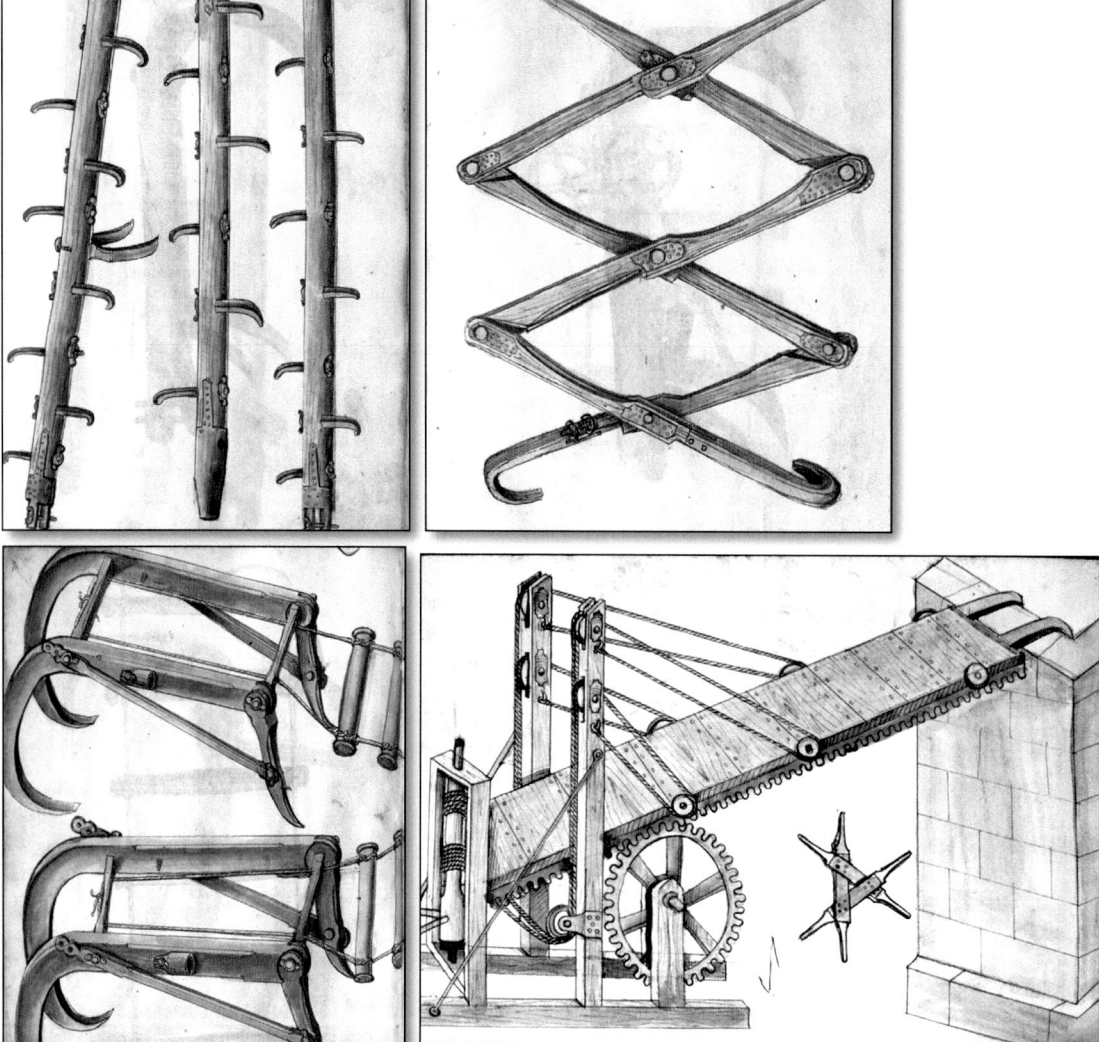

8.3. Siege Ladders. Source: Martin Merz *Feuerwerksbuch*. (BSB Cgm 599. Courtesy: Bayerische Staatsbibliothek)

Steding's men were chased from one street to the next and fought a rearguard action throughout the night having to contend with missiles of all descriptions being thrown at them by the women from the house windows above. Meanwhile, for the detachment which had made for the Cathedral square, Walter von Deventer was assigned the task of seizing the

---

Prophets and Preachers: Henry Gresbeck's Account of the Anabaptist Kingdom of Münster (Kirksville: Truman State University Press 2016), pp.273–274.

THE FINAL ASSAULT

cache of arquebuses stored in the minster while the rest of the men formed a dense battle line, unfurled their ensign, and struck up the drumbeat 'to arms'.[12] The defenders were quick to respond:

> Immediately, a great hue and cry arose that the enemy was operating in the middle of the city, had possession of the guns, and was marauding at will, killing and plundering. Roused from the streets, some hurriedly seized their arms to the extent that time allowed, some rushed unarmed from their houses and were cut down as they met the armed enemy, some unintentionally met with the guards left at the cathedral as they rushed in swarms to bring out the guns and were killed unawares. Realizing that the use of these guns had been taken from them, the armed men gathered in the marketplace and occupied the neighbouring Chapel of St Michael [Above the St Michael gate, the entrance to the Cathedral quarter – Author].[13]

With access to the arquebuses, Steding's men brought out the larger calibre pieces and used them to fire on the Anabaptists in the Chapel. However, the salvoes had little effect on the protective masonry. By now the defenders had armed themselves and charged across the square forcing the Bishop's men to regroup into a narrow alley across the square.[14]

> On the advice of Steding, however, a cannon opened a gate by force, and while the rest of the comrades were left there to bravely hold back the onslaught of the enemy, almost 200 escaped through the back doors into another street in the direction of the Church of St Giles. From there, they suddenly brought help to their hard-pressed comrades in a nearby alley, as if they were a new battle formation. Imagining that this was a new enemy force, the re-baptised (the defenders) began to get nervous, since they had no doubt that the whole city was in the hands of the enemy.[15]

---

12 Since Gresbeck remained outside the city during the action we must rely primarily on Kerssenbroch's account (pp.694–695) augmented by the less detailed accounts of two of the commanding officers – Justinian von Holzhausen and Graf Wirich von Dhaun, cf Documents 3 & 4 in the Appendix to Christopher Mackay, *False Prophets & Preachers: Henry Gresbeck's Account of the Anabaptist Kingdom of Münster*, (Kirksville: Truman State University Press, 2016), pp.288–295.
13 Hermann von Kerssenbroch, (Christopher S. Mackay tr.), *Narratio Historica Anabaptistici Furoris Monasterium*, (Narrative of the Anabaptist Madness. The overthrow of Münster, the Famous Metropolis of Westphalia) (Leiden–Boston: Brill 2007), pp.694–695.
14 Probably Pferdegeasse.
15 Christopher Mackay, *False Prophets & Preachers: Henry Gresbeck's Account of the Anabaptist Kingdom of Münster*, (Kirksville: Truman State University Press, 2016), Documents 3 & 4 in the Appendix, pp.288–295,

'A MIGHTY FORTRESS OF GOD': THE SIEGE OF MÜNSTER 1534-35

M.8. Section from the Alerdinck engraving showing the Jews' Field and Cross Gates – the major points of entry of the final assault. (Courtesy: Vermessungs- und Katasteramt Stadt Münster).

It was a chaotic scene. In the middle of the night van Leiden, woken by the alarm, sent a delegation across the square to broker a truce offering mercy to Steding's men who were still in battle formation, providing they laid down their weapons and surrendered. Steding refused and succeeded in despatching his ensign, von Twickel with the Colour hidden, and three other men from the rear of his square to the Jews' Field Gate to summon reinforcements. As dawn broke, von Twickel climbed on the rampart of the outer works and unfurled the banner[16] shouting to his fellow landsknechts below, 'Waldeck, Waldeck! Münster is ours! Fall in, fall in, our landsknechts!'[17]

There was some apprehension that this might be another Anabaptist ploy, but von Twickel shouted the password, *Maria*, and gained the trust of the assembled rank and file. It is not clear whether the ensign and his companions were responsible for the opening of the Jews' Field Gate which Graf Wirich von Dhaun stated in his report.[18] There is an account that the men used axes to break down the gate.[19] It may be assumed that the alarm having been raised, the watch at the gate had dispersed making the task of breaking down the gate achievable. Moreover, the moat at the Jews' Field Gate had been drained and crossing the stockade at this point in the absence of any resistance would also have been possible. Once the gate was opened, Dhaun and his men entered the city and made their way towards the Cathedral Square giving no quarter to any Anabaptist defender they encountered. As news spread that the Jews' Field Gate had been taken and that the Bishop's men were now pouring in, panic broke out amongst the defenders who were now fleeing in panic in all directions throughout the city.

Dhaun's main column of 3,000 landsknechts who had camped outside the city for sixteen months without booty, and some of whom had not been paid for two months, now wanted to take advantage of the situation. There

---

16   Twickel was in the Jülich contingent and may have borne the Jülich Banner.
17   Christopher Mackay, *False Prophets & Preachers: Henry Gresbeck's Account of the Anabaptist Kingdom of Münster*, (Kirksville: Truman State University Press, 2016), note 119; reported in a broadsheet in Hermann von Kerssenbroch, (Christopher S. Mackay tr.), *Narratio Historica Anabaptistici Furoris Monasterium*, (*Narrative of the Anabaptist Madness. The overthrow of Münster, the Famous Metropolis of Westphalia*) (Leiden–Boston: Brill 2007), p. 697.
18   Cf. Count Wirich von Falkenstein's account of the capture of Munster. Christopher Mackay, *False Prophets & Preachers: Henry Gresbeck's Account of the Anabaptist Kingdom of Münster*, (Kirksville: Truman State University Press, 2016), document 4 in the Appendix, pp.291-295. See also Letter from Marx Lesth von Molheim to Graf Philipp von Nassau in *Monatszeitschrift für die Geschichte Westdeutschlands* Vol. 5. 1879, p.230: *Doch zum letzten Haben sie mit derhulff Gottesdurchgeschlagen und die Pfort genannt Goedenfelt eingenommen und geöffnet...* (Finally with the help of God they fought through and took the gate known as the Jews' Field and opened it...)
19   'Wahrhaftiger Bericht der wunderbarlichen Handlung der Täufer in Münster Westfalen…' in *Westfälische Zeitschrift*, vol.33, 1875, p.13.

was no mercy for the defeated, although landsknecht convention spared pregnant women, childbearing women, and priests. One contemporary observer reported that the Bishop's men spent a day 'throttling' everyone they could find[20] and the streets were strewn with bodies.

Of the 800 to 900 Anabaptist defenders who had remained following the mass exodus during the months of April to June many were sick and weak from hunger. Van Leiden could muster only 200 to 250 men who were exempt from guard watch duty and had been kept relatively well fed.[21] Under the command of Henry Krechting these defenders had made a last stand in the circle of war wagons parked in the centre of the city. These

8.4. Gresbeck mentions an organ gun being on one of the war wagons which van Leiden commissioned. Also known as a *ribauldequin* this volley gun consisted of a number of small-calibre iron barrels set up parallel on a platform hence its resemblance to a pipe organ. Used from the late medieval period onwards its multiple barrels would discharge their projectiles at once, inflicting a lethal volley on a body of troops. Since organ guns were lighter, they could be carried on a wagon. It is not known whether such a piece from the city arsenal was mounted at the front of the war wagon, or if it was articulated in some way on the side of the wagon to swing in different directions as needs would have dictated. This example of a sixteenth century organ gun is based on a design by Michelangelo and consists of 12 barrels 66.5 cm long; it is capable of firing lead balls of between 16mm and 18 mm. It is currently on display at the Château de Castelnaud, France. (Photo: Sémhur via Wikimedia Commons)

---

20 'Wahrhaftiger Bericht der wunderbarlichen Handlung der Täufer in Münster Westfalen…' in *Westfälische Zeitschrift*, vol.33, 1875, p.13.
21 Karl-Heinz Kirchhoff, 'Die Belagerung und Eroberung Münsters 1534/35' in *Westfälische Zeitschrift* volume 112 (1962), p.142.

THE FINAL ASSAULT

wagons were well equipped with ordnance including arquebuses set up on the wagons to function as organ guns. Given such firepower there was a standoff between Dhaun's men and the defenders, however, this resistance was short lived.[22] Recognising Henry Krechting, Johann Raesfeld, one of Dhaun's commanders, made an approach and a negotiated surrender was achieved in which Krechting and 24 other Anabaptist defenders (most likely landsknechts) were granted immunity on condition they left the city; the remainder were however put to the sword.[23] At 6 pm on 25 June a rider was despatched to Bishop von Wolbeck to inform him that Münster had fallen.[24]

8.5. Cathedral Square today. (Photo: Jörg Schmalenberger, Wikimedia Commons)

---

22 Hermann von Kerssenbroch, (Christopher S. Mackay tr.), *Narratio Historica Anabaptistici Furoris Monasterium, (Narrative of the Anabaptist Madness. The overthrow of Münster, the Famous Metropolis of Westphalia)* (Leiden–Boston: Brill 2007), p.700.
23 Karl-Heinz Kirchhoff, 'Die Belagerung und Eroberung Münsters 1534/35' in *Westfälische Zeitschrift* volume 112 (1962), p.142.
24 Hermann von Kerssenbroch, (Christopher S. Mackay tr.), *Narratio Historica Anabaptistici Furoris Monasterium, (Narrative of the Anabaptist Madness. The overthrow of Münster, the Famous Metropolis of Westphalia)* (Leiden–Boston: Brill 2007), p.600.

9

Aftermath

Graf Dhaun reported that the carnage lasted until the evening of 26 June. One report gives 450 dead in the street fighting and 200 men slain in the houses afterwards. It was not until 27 June that the supreme commander ordered the slaughter to cease, and the remaining defenders be brought to the Cathedral Square.[1] The corpses of the starved and slain still lay in the alleys and in the houses. Summoned peasants buried the dead in mass graves. The number of Anabaptists killed cannot be precisely documented, since contemporary reports are very cautious on this point. One may assume that almost all able-bodied men were slain. Between 3,500 and 4,000 women survived the taking of the city.

The Bishop had given strict orders to take the important leaders prisoner. Bernd Krechting, the King's chancellor, was the first to be caught hiding in the Agidii Cloister along with Gerlach von Wullen, van Leiden's commander of the horse. Having sent delegates to undertake negotiations with Steding in the early hours and fearing the worst, the King had slipped away from the rear of his palace following an attempt by a soldier by the name of Röchell to apprehend him. Making his way to St Tilgen's Gate he was captured by Steding's men and delivered up to Graf Dhaun. Bernd Rothmann, who was a prime target for capture, was never found but it was generally thought that he had died in the fighting and that his corpse lay in amongst the many which were by now piling up.[2] Bernd Knipperdolling had been part of the fighting on the square but had hidden in a house by the

---

1 Karl-Heinz Kirchhoff, 'Die Belagerung und Eroberung Münsters 1534/35' in *Westfälische Zeitschrift* volume 112 (1962), p.143.
2 Rothmann's body was never found and his death in Münster could never be proved. According to a Fabricius Boland, who had visited Münster before 1546, the Münster physician Gerhard Marcellus had assured him that Rothmann had escaped and was living with a nobleman in Friesland to whom he had promised not to disturb the peace. Quoted in Karl-Heinz Kirchhoff, 'Die Belagerung und Eroberung Münsters 1534/35' in *Westfälische Zeitschrift* volume 112 (1962), p.43 (Internet-Portal *Westfälische Geschichte*).
URL: http://www.westfaelische-zeitschrift.lwl.org(accessed 16 August 2023).

New Bridge Gate. He was given up by its owner, a Catherine Hobbel who was granted immunity for doing so, although her husband succumbed to the same fate as the other able bodied Anabaptist defenders.[3]

One group of the Bishop's mercenaries had a more material preoccupation than searching for the leaders. This group of some 50 landsknechts, acting on information that there was a trove of gold and silver in the City Hall, raided the building. They were caught in the act and, since their actions contradicted the Bishop's articles of war, were taken to the cathedral square where their leaders were executed, and the rest sent in disgrace wearing nothing but their underclothes to the Cross Gate where they were banished from the city.[4]

Four days after the attack on 29 June Bishop von Waldeck rode into the city which by now had most of the corpses cleared away and buried. In the intervening days, the landsknechts had undertaken a house to house search for defenders still in hiding and any plunder. Given the losses they had incurred during 16 months of siege being picked off by sharpshooters and losing comrades in arms during the previous assaults, they were in no mood for leniency, dragging men out into the streets and killing them on the spot. Their searches of the city buildings uncovered a not insubstantial remaining supply of food in the royal court.[5]

Steding had sent two companies of men out to accompany his lord into Münster and on his arrival presented the Bishop with van Leiden's royal regalia as evidence of his victory. Three immediate issues prevented von Waldeck from basking in any glory: the question of booty and the payment of his landsknechts, deciding the fate of the surviving women in the city, and the processing of the Anabaptist leadership for punishment.

The Booty

The Bishop claimed half of the war booty and all the property of the Anabaptists in Münster as full booty (see Appendix I). His mercenaries were entitled to any removable possessions. Three booty masters (*Beutemeister*) from each company were appointed to note down all the household items they confiscated, and those expelled citizens were allowed to buy their

---

[3] Hermann von Kerssenbroch, (Christopher S. Mackay tr.), *Narratio Historica Anabaptistici Furoris Monasterium*, (*Narrative of the Anabaptist Madness. The overthrow of Münster, the Famous Metropolis of Westphalia*) (Leiden–Boston: Brill 2007), pp.703–704.

[4] Hermann von Kerssenbroch, (Christopher S. Mackay tr.), *Narratio Historica Anabaptistici Furoris Monasterium*, (*Narrative of the Anabaptist Madness. The overthrow of Münster, the Famous Metropolis of Westphalia*) (Leiden–Boston: Brill 2007), pp.703–704.

[5] Heinrich Gresbeck (Christopher S. Mackay trans. and added commentary), *False Prophets and Preachers: Henry Gresbeck's Account of the Anabaptist Kingdom of Münster* (Kirksville: Truman State University Press 2016), p.278.

property back. Everything else was sold by public auction and the proceeds designated as booty. The Bishop sequestrated not only the property but also any cannon which had been seized, leaving the supreme commander and the members of his council of war empty handed. Since the city had not been taken by an all-out assault but by a "clandestine attack", the bishop rejected Graf Dhaun's claim to one tenth of the spoils.[6] Contrary to expectations, the total booty was small. Each mercenary received only 16 or 18 Emden guilders. A booty inventory indicates 4,840 Guilders which were distributed to officers and captains of the horse (*Rittmeister*). The Bishop placed a value of 6 tuns of gold on the total booty. He himself despatched a chest of 450 pounds of unminted silver from the city. When the third month of the Worms relief ended on 2 July, some of the landsknechts still had not received their pay for a second month. There were ugly scenes.

Von Waldeck feared a mutiny and the departure of numbers of men into the service of Captain Ovelacker[7] who was recruiting on behalf of the city of Lübeck. To prevent this, he ordered his six captains of horse to be ready with their men to intervene. Matters were made worse by great unease within the Cathedral chapter and its members who were fearful of anarchy within the city and called on the Bishop to personally hire two companies of landsknechts at his own expense to maintain order. Thus, on 12 July, Wilken Steding and Egbert von Deveren were hired with two companies of men for three months. The remaining five companies were expected to stand down but were not prepared to leave the city until they had received their outstanding pay. Under these circumstances, the bishop had to cancel his participation at the meeting of princes in Essen scheduled for 9 July, fearing that mutiny would break out as soon as he left his see. As things happened serious unrest did break out on 18 July as von Waldeck departed for a meeting of the princes in Neuss.

> They wanted to kill all the *Beutemeister*, as well as all the captains, and to plunder the city one more time, and to sell the goods. Once they held the assembly, they had the *Beutemeister* come into the centre ....[8] and asked them if they knew of more gold. The *Beutemeister* said no, they couldn't get more gold together than what amounted to a half ton of so that each landsknechts received sixteen Emden guilders as booty. The landsknechts had two of the *Beutemeister* racked on the ladder by the hangman, so that they would say where the gold now was. [However] they couldn't get any information out of them.[9]

---

6 Heinrich Gresbeck (Christopher S. Mackay trans. and added commentary), *False Prophets and Preachers: Henry Gresbeck's Account of the Anabaptist Kingdom of Münster* (Kirksville: Truman State University Press 2016), p.278.
7 Eberhard Ovelacker had been dismissed from the Bishop's service in December and had entered the service of Christoph von Oldenburg
8 The ring was the main decision-making body within a landsknecht army.
9 Heinrich Gresbeck (Christopher S. Mackay trans. and added commentary), *False*

After his return from Neuß, the Bishop paid the mercenaries, with each man receiving 16 Emden guilders from his own booty of 26,000 Gg. and gave Steding the task of thanking his infantry. At the end of July the Bishop was able to inform his councillors in Worms that he had succeeded in persuading the 5 companies to leave the city. However, his financial obligations were by now enormous (see Appendix IV).[10]

The Fate of the Women

On 5 July all the women were summoned to the cathedral square. The non-natives of the city were to be expelled while those native Münster women who could find a guarantor to prove their innocence were pardoned and allowed to remain in the city. When, however, most of them refused to renounce their faith, the "most distinguished" were arrested and punished. This included Divara – the former widow of Jan Matthijs and now Jan van Leiden's 'Queen' who was executed along with four other women. The others were expelled from the city. One year later, a register records 216 women and 19 men living in Münster who had renounced Anabaptism and had provided a guarantor who could vouch for their innocence.[11]

Punishment of the Leadership

Jan van Leiden, Bernd Knipperdolling and Bernd Krechting were held in captivity in cells in the Rosenthal church. Van Leiden was paraded in chains to meet the bishop and endure the ignominy of seeing his regalia handed over to von Waldeck. In a typical defiant stance, when the Bishop sarcastically asked him 'And are you a King? Van Leiden responded 'And are you a Bishop?[12] Whilst execution of the ringleaders would be a foregone conclusion the authorities wanted to implement due process.

Gerlach von Wullen, one of Jan van Leiden's two military commanders, was released following interventions by his aristocratic relatives, but Christian Kerckerinck, supervisor of the city defences, was summarily executed. The three main prisoners were detained for a further 6 months

---

Prophets and Preachers: Henry Gresbeck's Account of the Anabaptist Kingdom of Münster (Kirksville: Truman State University Press 2016), pp.280–281.

10 Karl-Heinz Kirchhoff, 'Die Belagerung und Eroberung Münsters 1534/35' in *Westfälische Zeitschrift* volume 112 (1962), pp.146-149.

11 Karl-Heinz Kirchhoff, 'Die Belagerung und Eroberung Münsters 1534/35' in *Westfälische Zeitschrift* volume 112 (1962), p.144

12 *Heinrich Gresbeck* (Christopher S. Mackay trans. and added commentary), *False Prophets and Preachers: Henry Gresbeck's Account of the Anabaptist Kingdom of Münster* (Kirksville: Truman State University Press 2016), p.281. Without having taken holy orders von Waldeck received numerous canonships, in Cologne, Trier, Mainz and Paderborn, despite having not been ordained at the time.

'A MIGHTY FORTRESS OF GOD': THE SIEGE OF MÜNSTER 1534-35

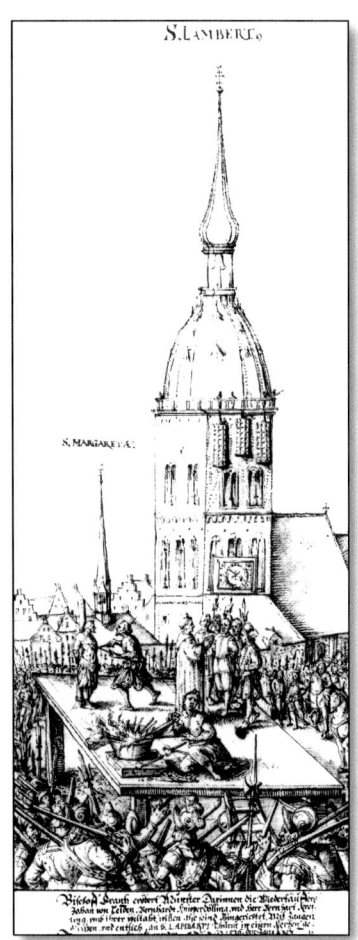

during which time a team of inquisitors led by Antonius Corvinus, a Lutheran theologian, were charged with the task of not only persuading them of the errors of their ways, thereby allowing them to recant, but also of extracting the names of their associates in the major cities of north-west Germany and The Netherlands. Records show a series of interrogations of each leader including torture (*peinliches Verhör*) but they were unsuccessful in achieving the disclosure of any names or whereabouts of their allies in other cities.[13] They were paraded in rolling cages throughout the countryside before being brought back to Münster in January 1536 for execution. Sentenced to death for introducing a forbidden religion, desecrating churches, theft, agitating against the government, establishing a kingdom, murder, and numerous other offences, their execution was a particularly painful one. The dead bodies, each bound in a standing position, were hung in iron cages from St Lambert's tower.

9.1. Sentenced to death, Jan van Leiden, Bernd Knipperdolling and the councillor Bernd Krechting were executed in accordance with the provisions of the *Peinliche Halsgerichtsordnung* of 1531 on 22 January 1536, on the Prinzipalmarkt in Münster. The death sentence was carried out in accordance with the specific provisions of the punishment for sedition. Each of the three was attached to a pole by an iron spiked collar and his body ripped with red-hot tongs for an hour. After this their tongues were pulled out with tongs before each was killed with a burning dagger thrust through the heart. A historical depiction dating to 1607 of the execution of the Anabaptists showing the cages already suspended on the old tower of the Lamberti Church. (Artist unknown. Public domain)

In an effort to recover part of his war expenses, Bishop Franz von Waldeck confiscated the houses of Münster Anabaptists; but their sale brought little income, since the houses in the city were generally burdened with mortgages, which lessened their worth. Bishop von Waldeck recatholicised Münster and determined the members of the city council who sat from 1536 onwards. Not until 1554 were the citizens able to elect their council again.

Even before the executions Franz von Waldeck had to make strategic decisions about the reestablishment of political and religious order both in the city and in his bishopric. The meetings of the Imperial Circle at Koblenz and Worms had expressly reserved the right to determine the new order in Münster following the capitulation of the Anabaptists. The Bishop, however, who had, along with his estates, borne the brunt of the war, was not willing, following this hard-won success, to have such matters placed

---

13 Richard van Dülmen, *Das Täuferreich zu Münster 1534-1535: Berichte und Dokumente* (Munich Deutscher Taschenbuch Verlag, 1974), pp.264–280.

AFTERMATH

in the hands of the Circle. His plan was to build a fortress in the city and thereby consolidate his rule within the city and the bishopric. The Landgraf von Hessen was the first of the allies to agree to these plans. However, these agreements were to come at a price – granting permission for Lutheran preachers to return to the city.[14]

The Bishop's message to the Prince Electors of the lower Rhine was that to keep the city of Münster in obedience to the bishop and The Empire, no better means could be found, than to lay down in Münster 'the most important fortresses as the strongest bulwarks, ramparts and fortifications' and to leave the city with only walls and towers. Otherwise, it was to be feared that the mercenaries or the pardoned citizens might 'place such a fortified town into the hands of a foreigner' or cause a new uprising, which, given the strong fortifications, would be difficult to counter. This plan did not correspond at all to the wishes of the princes, who decided at the assembly in Neuss to take the city's fortifications down. At the meeting of the Imperial Circle in Worms on 18 July, they tried to dissuade the bishop by raising serious concerns. To build a 'fortress' in Münster would be lengthy, expensive, and dangerous; it would damage the privileges of the city and require the prior permission of the parties involved including the Hanseatic League and other cities. It was therefore more advisable that the 'outermost and most noble fortress be demolished, the ramparts razed, and the ditches filled in.' Both the Prince Elector of Trier and Herzog von Cleves were particularly in favour of this proposal.[15] Since the assembly closed without coming to a definitive resolution on the matter of a new order for the city and the bishopric, Bishop von Waldeck had gained time to implement his plans.

After the departure of the majority of the Bishop's landsknechts at the end of July 1535, two companies remained as a garrison and the blockhouses

9.2. After the gruesome execution, the three mutilated corpses were put in cages and hung from the tower of St Lambert's church as a deterrent to heretics. About fifty years later the bones were removed, but the cages, after periodic restoration, remain in place today. (Photo: Lyndal Roper and author)

---

14 Karl-Heinz Kirchhoff, 'Die Belagerung und Eroberung Münsters 1534/35' in *Westfälische Zeitschrift* volume 112 (1962), p.150.
15 Karl-Heinz Kirchhoff, 'Die Belagerung und Eroberung Münsters 1534/35' in *Westfälische Zeitschrift* volume 112 (1962), p.158.

and redoubts continued to be guarded. As late as September nothing was allowed into the city until it could be made safe. The two company commanders exercised day to day control until they were replaced by Bernd von Oer who assumed the governorship on behalf of the Bishop on 1 November. At a meeting of the *Landtag* (regional council) at Dülmen on 25 July 1535, the estates approved the construction of two fortresses in Münster, and as early as 1 August, peasants were to rebuild the *Zwinger* and the *Neuwerk*, as two heavily fortified bastions.[16] By late autumn the Bishop had achieved his goal – under the strict control of his governor, Münster was now firmly in the hands of its Prince-Bishop. Now it was a matter of defending the position gained against the expected protests of the Imperial Circle.

On 13 March 1536 Imperial commissioners arrived in Münster to monitor the implementation of the provisions they believed had been agreed at a subsequent meeting of the Circle at Worms during the previous November. They concluded that the draft of the 'New Order' for the city was 'quite repugnant and contrary' to what had been agreed. Unable to resolve the matter with the Bishop they departed again on 23 March paving the way for the Bishop and the estates of his territory to declare his 'New Order' for the city on 30 April 1536.

On 4 May, the Bishop established the new magistrate and accepted the oath of allegiance from the citizens of Münster. In the same month, the construction of the new fortress on the *Neuwerk*, later called *Engelsburg*, began. However, a year later the construction of the *Engelsburg* still remained unfinished and two years later the *Zwinger* and the St Aegidii were relinquished as his personal fortresses. His governorship of the city ended on 5 August following the Imperial restitution of Catholicism in the city on 5 August 1541. Following the lifting of the ban on the guilds, Emperor Karl V reinstated all the old privileges on 26 July 1553, heralding the first successful act of the Counter Reformation in Germany.[17]

Anabaptism Beyond Münster

The fall of Münster in 1535 did not mark the end of Anabaptism. Widespread activity by its survivors was impossible due to the death of almost all the men in the city. However, the small group of defenders who had been released along with Heinrich Krechting was able to engage in some activity under the protection of the Graf von Oldenburg, an enemy of the Prince-Bishop. They were assisted in their task by a number of the women who had

---

16   Karl-Heinz Kirchhoff, 'Die Belagerung und Eroberung Münsters 1534/35' in *Westfälische Zeitschrift* volume 112 (1962), p.159. In May 1536, the construction of a third fortress, the so-called *Engelsburg*, began on the site of the *Neuwerk*.
17   Karl-Heinz Kirchhoff, 'Die Belagerung und Eroberung Münsters 1534/35' in *Westfälische Zeitschrift* volume 112 (1962), p.166.

been expelled from Münster. In the confession of the Netherlander Jan van Batenburg he claimed that among the Anabaptists in Oldenburg was 'the baptiser Bernadus, a great man who came out of Münster,' which suggests that Rothmann may have survived.[18] In villages and farming communities, the wandering preachers found a welcome reception and refuge, so that soon a network of secret connections once again spanned the country.[19]

For the Melchiorites in Amsterdam, the capitulation of Münster forced them to undertake a reappraisal of their faith, culminating in three new strands epitomised in the spiritualism of Obbe Philips and David Joris, the radical militantism of Jan van Batenburg[20] and the more pacifist directions of Menno Simons and Dirk Philips,[21] which can still be found in the Mennonite, Amish, and Hutterite communities of the world today.

---

18 Ralf Klötzer, 'The Melchiorites in Münster' in Stayer, James, Roth, John (Eds.) *A Companion to Anabaptism and Spiritualism, 1521-1700* (Leiden: Brill, 2006), p.250.
19 Karl-Heinz Kirchhoff, 'Die Belagerung und Eroberung Münsters 1534/35' in *Westfälische Zeitschrift* volume 112 (1962), p.43.
20 In 1537, Jan van Batenburg, one of the instigators of the notorious attack of 1535 on the Oldeklooster, planned to capture a city in The Netherlands in an attempt to imitate the formation of the Kingdom of Münster. His impact was short lived; he was arrested in 1537 and executed a year later. cf. John M. McLaughlin, *Factors of religious violence and a path to peace: a study of the 16th century Anabaptists.*, unpublished M.A. in Defence Analysis, Norwich University 2015, pp.31-33.
21 Gary K Waite, 'The Anabaptist Movement in Amsterdam and the Netherlands, 1531-1535: An Initial Investigation into its Genesis and Social Dynamics', *The Sixteenth Century Journal*, vol. 18, No.2 (Summer, 1987), p.264.

10

Conclusion

The events during the sixteen months of the siege of Münster have led one commentator to describe the Anabaptist commune as a 'proto-communist, polygamous, theocratic, doomsday sex cult governed through fear and violence.'[1] This is by no means an uncommon judgement as the general historiography reveals. However, considered from a military history perspective, the Anabaptist commune can only be judged against the perpetual state of war it found itself in. Most of the leadership decisions, it could be argued, were dictated by the necessities of war.[2] Regardless of religious ideology, the pressing political situation of besieged Münster created conditions which lent themselves to extreme alterations of societal structure. Food shortages, military organization, internal cohesion, and religious conformity all provided political challenges for the Anabaptist leadership.[3] It is interesting to speculate whether, under a regime of religious tolerance and an absence of a siege, such events would have come to pass within the city. The destruction of the city's churches and the willingness of the citizens of Münster to fight to the last man or woman in defence of their 'holy' city indicate that establishing and maintaining a place which sixteenth century Anabaptists could call their own and in which they could shape their living was of primary and not secondary importance.[4]

Much vilified for his role in the Münster commune, Jan van Leiden had the task of filling the vacuum left by the unexpected death of Matthijs and by dint of his charisma was able to maintain the morale of the besieged populace until starvation brought on by the Bishop's blockade severely

---

1   Paul D. Wilke, https://www.steelsnowflake.org/post/munster-rebellion (accessed 20 August 2023).
2   http://www.allempires.com/allempires.com-redirect/article/index.php?q=anabaptist_commune_munster (accessed 12 August 2023).
3   Darren T. Williamson, '"For the Honor Of God And To Fulfil His Will": The Role Of Polygamy in Anabaptist Münster' in *Restoration Quarterly,* Volume 1.1. 2000, p.30.
4   Henry Suderman, 'Sometimes it's the Place: the Anabaptist Kingdom Revisited' *Renaissance and Reformation*, volume 40 no.4, 2017, p.140.

CONCLUSION

undermined their determination. Moreover, he proved himself to be a worthy commander of a besieged city until treachery coupled with starvation forced the capitulation of the Anabaptist resistance.

For the modern-day reader, with or without religious conviction, it might seem inconceivable that the decision to adopt a specific religious faith at the right time in an individual's life, could result in the systematic extermination of the followers holding such a belief. By any reckoning, the characterisation of the Anabaptist commune of Münster as an episode of religious mania, whether or not brought about by the exigencies of defending a siege, pales into insignificance against the backdrop of the state terrorism which resulted in the persecution and deaths of thousands of innocent Anabaptist believers throughout much of the sixteenth century and beyond.

Colour Plate Commentaries

Plate A. Everard Alerdinck's Map of Münster.

Map by Everhard Alerdinck (1598–1658) completed in 1636 and purporting to represent a bird's eye view of Munster at the time. This represents a Vauban style of fortification and is not to scale so that the outer rings look much wider than they were. Since fortifications were in a state of constant construction at the time of the siege, some parts of the outer walls and bastions would have appeared somewhat more rudimentary, cf image in Chapter 2. (Reproduced courtesy of Heinrich Guttermann, Vermessungs und Katasteramt Stadt Münster).

Plate B. Jan van Leiden, and Gatekeeper

1. Jan van Leiden is depicted wearing a suit of armour, likely as worn during his appearance at drills and when inspecting the defences. According to Gresbeck, he clothed himself:

> magnificently along with his servants and he had himself made a velvet coat, and magnificent hose and doublet of magnificent silk work, and a magnificent golden cap, and a velvet bonnet with a crown, and a sword with a golden sheath, and an armour dagger with a golden sheath, and many golden chains, which he wore around his neck. What the King had on his horse – the equipment and trappings – was also all covered with gold. For I hold that there was silver on the trappings, and it was gilded. The King also had two gilded spurs. I also hold that these too were made of silver and gilded over.[1]

---

1   *Heinrich Gresbeck* (Christopher S. Mackay trans. and added commentary), *False Prophets and Preachers: Henry Gresbeck's Account of the Anabaptist Kingdom of Münster* (Kirksville: Truman State University Press 2016), p.140.

It may well have been pure gold. He is depicted wearing a half suit of armour based on that on display in the City Museum, Münster.

2. Gatekeeper. The King immediately liveried his servants with hose clearly distinguished crosswise red and grey, the one red and the other grey and on their sleeves – The King had the gatekeeper in front of each gate, and they too had a distinctive livery, also red covered with grey trim. This figure is wearing a typical coat with skirts with a key stitched on one sleeve so that they would remember to unlock and lock the gates.[2] Servants also wore a gold ring on their finger the value of which varied according to their rank. This figure is impart based on a reconstruction featured in the book 'The King's Servants: men's dress at the accession of Henry VIII' by Caroline Johnson.

Plate C. Artillery

1. Heavy artillery piece. The Bishop had to acquire his siege artillery on loan from his allies. As was the custom, many pieces were christened by their gunmakers. Many of these names were already known to the defenders. *The Devil* and *His Mother*, the *Whore of Babylon*, the *Flying Spirit*, and the *Snake* (culverin) *of Zwolle* to name a few.[3]

2. & 4. Siege Cannon and hoist. The barrels, generally too heavy to be mounted on a wheeled carriage would be brought to the siegeworks separately and then lifted into position using a form of crane winch. Usually these would be located on an incline chosen by the master gunner to ensure maximum trajectory with a series of wooden posts and boards to the rear to take the recoil of each shot.

3. Mortar. Mortars were particularly favoured in siege work for their high, curved trajectory firing and came in a variety of calibres. They propelled stone balls, solid iron shot, or incendiary devices over the city walls. Some projectiles could be designed to explode in the air thus showering the defenders below with metal fragments. The powder chamber of a mortar was specially designed to concentrate the charge in a small area so that the projectile would receive as much of explosion's propulsive force as possible. (Zeugbuch Kaiser Maximilians BSB Cod. Icon. 222. Courtesy of Bayerische Staatsbibliothek).

---

2   *Heinrich Gresbeck* (Christopher S. Mackay trans. and added commentary), *False Prophets and Preachers: Henry Gresbeck's Account of the Anabaptist Kingdom of Münster* (Kirksville: Truman State University Press 2016), p.139.

3   Hermann von Kerssenbroch, (Christopher S. Mackay tr.), *Narratio Historica Anabaptistici Furoris Monasterium*, (*Narrative of the Anabaptist Madness. The overthrow of Münster, the Famous Metropolis of Westphalia*) (Leiden–Boston: Brill 2007), p.574.

Plate D. Explosive Devices

Franz Helm (*c.* 1500–1567) was an artillery master who lived and worked in Southern Germany in the first half of the sixteenth century. Born in Cologne, he wrote a comprehensive description of what an ideal arsenal might look like and this exists in manuscript as 'Das Buch von den Probierten Künsten' ('Book of the practical arts'). These "novel" and "superior" examples, which would have had direct use in defending a siege, reveal methods which have survived to this day.
1. exploding barrel with metal inserts, f.61r.
2. grenades containing barbs and iron spikes, f.95v.
3. exploding wheels, f.87r.
4. early forms of Molotov cocktails containing gunpowder, f.47r.
5. exploding tree stumps, f.91v. A hollowed-out tree trunk, shod with iron bands and iron spikes, to hold powder. Flames are already coming out of three openings. Overlaid: 'A storm block with shot.' Below, another shod tree trunk is about to explode, causing the pebble charge to shoot out on both sides, tearing open the tree wall and causing flames to emerge.
6. Improvised incendiary devices using pitchers, f.100r.
7. Arrow with incendiary device wrapped in a bag, f.90v.

Source: Franz Helm, 'Buch der probierten Künsten 1535', Heidelberg University Library, Cod. Pal. Germ. 128.

Plate E. Handgunner, cavalryman, and female defender

1. Anabaptist handgunner, April 1535

The hand gunner is holding a 'double hook', so-called because its length was twice that of a normal matchlock with the barrel bearing a hook for steadying the weapon on a parapet or palisade. By this time bandoliers bearing 12 wooden 'apostles' were becoming more standard. In addition, the gunner carried a ball bag made of leather with balls weighing about 30 grams, a small vial of fine powder ("match") for the primer, a tin vial with oil for greasing the plugs, the folded fuse – a hemp rope soaked in lead acetate that could glow for hours, and a small spike for cleaning the ignition hole.

2. Member of the King's horse troop

Van Leiden had two troops of horse – one armed with lances, the other with firearms. This cavalryman is carrying a short lance. The king's knights were recognised by their unique and special clothing which was made mismatched [asymmetrical] thus these half jackets had one arm without a sleeve and half the chest without skirts so that although it was knightly it was also skimpy (or flimsy) and is here shown worn over a suit of half armour. Gresbeck describes how the court/household servants were dressed in red coats decorated with grey piping (lace trim) and for each had a sleeve embroidered with a globe, similar to the other clothing of the king's retinue, i.e. pierced by two swords.[4] We can assume that the King's cavalry also wore this device on their left sleeve.

3. Female defender

In the first half of the sixteenth century, German women's dress varied widely from that worn in other parts of Europe, with skirts cut separately from bodices. In this case the defender is wearing a loose, linen undershirt. The skirt, hitched up at the hips to allow better movement, has a high waistline, a feature of dress in The Netherlands and Flanders. Hair was more often worn uncovered, braided, or twisted with ribbons and pinned up, or confined in a net. The Birgitta Cap fashioned from a length of white linen was a common form of headgear amongst the lower classes. Gresbeck describes how a company of women assembled at the muster in the cathedral square with some armed with a 'handled pike' which was probably an *Aalspiess* (eel pike) as shown here.

Plate F. Banners

There is little information in the eyewitness accounts about details of the banners which are mentioned. The banners and heraldry in the plate relate to known contingents and/or individuals who fought in the siege.
1. Banner of Cologne
2. Banner of Cleves
3. Banner of the city of Meissen
4. Coat of Arms of von Waldeck
5. Heraldic sign of the Steding family
6. Coat of Arms of Graf Wirich von Dhaun

---

4   I am grateful to Jane Malcolm-Davies of 'The Tudor Tailor' for assistance in providing background clothing information and for translating Gresbeck's description of the cavalry clothing.

'A MIGHTY FORTRESS OF GOD': THE SIEGE OF MÜNSTER 1534-35

Plate G. Landsknecht Archer, Sapper, Standard Bearer

1. Landsknecht Archer

Although archers had become almost redundant on the field of battle being essentially replaced with the introduction of firearms, their skill was used during sieges where the arquebus had little impact against a parapet. A bow could deliver smaller missiles including incendiary devices over the city walls.

Details based on a coloured drawing from the Zeugbuch Kaiser Maximilians, (Cod. Icon 222, Bayerische Staatsbibliothek).

2. Sapper

Most of the siege works, including trenches and ramparts, were undertaken by peasants pressed into service by the Bishop's pressure on his vassals. This man is pushing a wheelbarrow used either for moving earth away or carrying stone cannonballs to the heavier artillery pieces.

3. Ensign Guelders Contingent

The standard bearer is wearing the so-called Spanish influenced *Pumphose* or round hose which was becoming the fashion at this time. We know this because Matthäus Schwarz (19 February 1497–c.1574) whom we might call the first male fashionista of his age, chronicled the clothing he wore between 1520 and 1560 in his 'Book of Clothing'[5]. His entry for 1535 shows him wearing this baggy 'round' hose over his leggings. Landsknecht clothing began to adopt this style before morphing into the entirely impractical *Pluderhose* later in the century.

Plate H. The Siege

This view of the siege of the city defended by the Anabaptists against the army of the Prince-Bishop and his allies is not an exact representation, but it may have been composed based on sketches and written reports. Recognizable are the location at the River Aa, which flows diagonally through the picture, the hills with the burning windmills, the double ditch with the outer rampart. Inside the city, the Town Hall is sketchily recognizable, in front of it an execution scene; in the centre, a church tower

---

5   Philippe Braunstein, *Unbanquiermis a nu : Autobiographie de Matthäus Schwarz, bourgeois d'Augsbourg. Découvertes Gallimard Albums* (Paris: Éditions Gallimard, 1992).

used as a watchtower – designed almost like a crossing tower and probably drawn together from the Ludgeri and Lamberti churches; on the right, the destroyed cathedral and the church above the water with a dropped spire and a gun emplacement on the tower. It seems as if the internal drawing of the city is laid out laterally reversed. Numerous military actions and actors are depicted around the city.
(Erhard Schön (1491–1542), the Siege of Münster 1534, courtesy: LWL-Museum für Kunst und Kultur, Westfälisches Landesmuseum, Münster)

Appendix I

The Bishop's Articles of War

1) Upon taking the oath every soldier shall, wherever the need arises, fight the Bishop's enemy bravely without flinching and shall protect the prince and his subjects with all their might.
2) Soldiers in the service of the Bishop are expected to uphold all the customary articles of military discipline as befits proper, upright soldiers.
3) All cities, strongholds, guns, gunpowder, shot, shall upon capture become the property of the Bishop.
4) The Bishop is not obliged to pay his soldiers any siege bonus if he permits them to engage in plunder.
5) The council chamber is not to be plundered or in any way violated by the officers and their men and is to be left intact for the Prince. The Prince also hereby lays claim to one half of all other plunder.
6) Those knights, prelates and citizens forced to leave the city shall be given priority in purchasing back their property.
7) Following the capture of the city nothing affixed to a wall or the grounds of a property is to be removed.
8) Once the city is captured by the grace of God, the soldiers will turn over control of all the city gates and fortifications to the Prince or to those appointed by him.
9) Following the taking of the city through the grace of God, the soldiers shall depart within eight days at the drum signal. During this time, they shall divide and sell their booty. Any outstanding wages owed by the Bishop shall be duly paid out.
10) Neither officers nor rank and file shall kill any rebel leaders captured during the storming of the city (their names will be drawn up in a careful list). As far as possible, they are to be spared and brought to the Prince in exchange for a handsome reward.

Appendix II

The first Ordinance introduced by the twelve elders for the political government in the city of Münster[1]

Those called upon through the grace of the highest, all-powerful God and established as the elders of the community of Christ in the saintly city of Münster wish the following duties and articles to be upheld faithfully and without violation by the individual inhabitants of Israel and of the house of God.

1) Each Israelite will obey whatever Holy Scripture either orders or prohibits through fear of punishment.
2) Each individual will devote himself zealously to his own calling, fearing God and the ruler established by Him. For the latter does not wear the sword in vain, being the avenger of crimes.
3) Each of the elders will employ the services of one attendant to carry out his commands.
4) Five of the elders will be in command of the day and of the night watches and will conduct a personal inspection to make sure that the community receives no harm through the carelessness of the watchman.
5) Every night, one more of the elders will, with a few armed attendants, carefully examine the watchmen on duty on the ramparts and walls and at the gates in order that they should be kept to their duty and that God should keep watch with them.

---

[1] Hermann von Kerssenbroch, (Christopher S. Mackay tr.), *Narratio Historica Anabaptistici Furoris Monasterium*, (*Narrative of the Anabaptist Madness. The overthrow of Münster, the Famous Metropolis of Westphalia*) (Leiden–Boston: Brill 2007), pp.550–553.

6) Every day from 6 until 8 o'clock in the morning and from 1 until 3 o'clock in the afternoon, six elders will sit in a place assigned to them in the market and settle all disputes with their decisions.

7) Whatever the elders will decide by their common judgment to be beneficial in this new community of Israel, John of Leiden the prophet will, as a faithful minister and ruler of the highest and sacrosanct God, announce and explain this to the community of Christ and to the entire assembly of Israel.

8) To make sure that no manifest crime which conflicts with the Word of God is tolerated among the sincere and by no means fraudulent Israelites, and that the transgressor criminal who is caught in a crime red-handed should be subjected to the worthy punishment, Bernd Knipperdolling the sword bearer will punish such a criminal in accordance with the crime which he has committed. If, on the other hand, he is not caught red-handed, Knipperdolling will refer the matter to the elders, and their decision will be complied with, so that every evil will be eradicated from Israel. To protect and defend his office, Knipperdolling will go forth in public with an escort of four attendants.

9) In order to preserve the lawful order in serving food, every day those superintending this matter will, with due regard for their duty, set dishes of the same kind (as has generally been the practice hitherto) before the brothers and sisters as they sit modestly and with all decorum at separate tables. The diners will not have the discretion to ask for anything beyond what is set before them. [2]

10) Those who in the meanwhile keep the watch during the day will have their meal when the others have gone their way, so that the necessary keeping of the watch is not neglected.

11) No one will fish apart from the superintendents of fishing, Christian Kerckering and Herman Redeker, and their attendants, who will also not deny fish to the sick and pregnant in accordance with their needs.

12) Bernd Boentruppe and Gerard Pruessen will have control over slaughtering, curing and selling meat, so that there will be no shortage of fresh meat at appropriate moments.

13) Herman tor Nate, John Redeker and Henry Dumkuster will, with their six servants, sew shoes for the use of the Israelites.

---

2   Hermann von Kerssenbroch, (Christopher S. Mackay tr.), *Narratio Historica Anabaptistici Furoris Monasterium*, (*Narrative of the Anabaptist Madness. The overthrow of Münster, the Famous Metropolis of Westphalia*) (Leiden–Boston: Brill 2007), pp.550–553. In front of each city gate, they had a house in which those working on strengthening the defences would have their meal at their assigned time. There were both men and women among them, and they would sit in silence at the table while eating as one of them read from the Old Testament.

THE FIRST ORDINANCE INTRODUCED BY THE TWELVE ELDERS

14) The blacksmiths John Palck, Henry Pothof, Henry Stolte, Conrad Pothof, Herman Berning, and Arnold Rodtland will deny their services to no one. Mollenhecke and Steinkamp, on the other hand, will serve only the government in forging iron.
15) John of Coesfeld will, with his servants, forge iron nails.
16) Bernard tor Moer, Bernard Glandorp, Henry Edelblot and John Northof will be the superintendents of clothes menders, and will see to it that no new and unusual varieties of clothing are made.
17) No one will wear torn or rent clothing.
18) Henry Krechting will, as notary and secretary, write down the secret counsels and the public and private decisions of the elders.
19) Henry Mollenhecke and Bernard, the clothing cutter will make sure that nothing required for the guns and artillery and their usage is lacking.
20) In order that wine and other varieties of aged drink should be preserved for the use of the sick and those in mental distress, Stephen Kopperschleger will undertake a careful accounting of this matter.
21) In order that gold and silver, both minted and not, should be put to proper and lawful use, Magnus Koehus, Conrad Kruse, Gerard Reining, and Lucas Gruter will make sure with extraordinary care that none will be spent uselessly and that it will be put to use for the general good through the planning of the elders.
22) Andrew the tanner and Herman Ribbert will superintend the preparation of tanned hides and whatever pertains to shoe making in this saintly community.
23) Eberhard Follen and John Krechting will be veterinarians and will oversee the horses assigned to public service in order to make sure that fodder is not used up without benefit.
24) Gerard Kibbenbrock, Christian Wordeman, John of Deventer, and John Uldan will see to strengthening or building anew the public defences of this saintly city. They will, however, build nothing without consulting the elders.
25) John Krechting will convey any turnip seeds that he finds in the city to the oil press and will faithfully keep the oil pressed from them for necessary uses.
26) Bernard Menneken will bring the spices and loaves of sugar to one house and superintend them, making sure that they are distributed properly
27) Whenever beer and bread are necessary, the elders will, by the grace of God, see to it that no harm comes to the community
28) Whenever earth is needed to repair the ramparts, Derek Schloschen will acquire two-horse and four-horse wagons for this purpose, and he will order the copper, lead and pewter to be removed from the thrown down towers and conveyed to separate piles for each.
29) If a foreigner not belonging to our religion, whether he is a brother or a fellow burgher of the same homeland or an acquaintance, has come to our saintly city, he will be turned over to Knipperdolling, the

sword bearer, for examination, so that Knipperdolling will engage him in conversation, which will be revealed to no one but the elders.

30) In order to avoid any suspicion of conspiracy, no baptised Christian will have a conversation or discussion with any foreign immigrant unbeliever or take any food with him.

31) No one will engage in fishing through any craft at all, subject to the penalty laid out for disobedience.

32) Under penalty of death no one will, without the consent and decision of the elders, change his company or transfer from one platoon to another at his own discretion.

33) If, by God's ordinance, someone dies by being shot by the enemy or for any other reason, no one will, by his own authority, assume the property that he leaves behind such as weapons, clothing and so on. Instead, the property will be taken to Bernd Knipperdolling the sword bearer, who will present it to the elders, so that it will be assigned to the true heirs by their authority.

Appendix III

List of officers of the court as decreed by Jan von Leiden[1]

1.	Bernd Knipperdolling	Governor/Mayor
2.	Bernd Rothmann	Preacher (Worthalter)
3.	Gert tom Kloster	} Councillors
4.	Bernd Krechting	}
5.	Heinrich Redeker	}
6.	Gerhard Reyninck	}
7.	Johann Kursener	Captain of the horse
8.	Hermann Tilbeck	Court master
9.	Gerlach von Wullen	} Commanders
10.	Lambert von Lueck	}
11.	Heinrich Krechting	Chancellor
12.	Johann Puchmann	Secretary
13.	Andreas von Coesfeld	Magistrate
14.	Gert Kippenbroick	Master of the credence table
15.	Bernd von Zwolle	Chief cook
16.	Walter Schenking	Cup bearer
17.	Evert Reimensnider	Tailor
18.	Kort Kruse	Commanding officer
19.	Gert von Bonn	Gatekeeper

---

1 Richard Van Dülmen, *Das Täuferreich zu Münster 1534-1535: Berichte und Dokumente* (Munich Deutscher Taschenbuch Verlag, 1974), des Münsterischen Königs Jan van Leiden Hofordnung (1534–5) pp.154– 157.

20.	Johann Ossenbeck	}	Vintners
21.	Johann Salwiede	}	
22.	Cornelius Keisepreister		Supervisor of wood supplies
23.	Bernd Boentrupp	}	Butchers
24.	Gert Prüsse	}	
25.	Henry Sanctes	}	Armourers
26.	Johann Middelbur	}	
27.	Christian Kerkerinck	}	Builders
28.	Johann Kerkerinck	}	
29.	Gert Mackenborg	}	
30.	Johann von Deventer	}	
31.	Anton Grotevader	}	
32.	Gert von Oldensell	}	Bodyguards
33.	Quirin von Lecker	}	
34.	Hermann von Billerbeck	}	
35.	Johann Voß	}	
36.	Ernst vom Damme	}	
37.	Johann von Greven	}	
38.	Engelbert Edinck	}	
39.	Jürgen Fromme	}	
40.	Anton Velthues	}	
41.	Egbert Scharlaken	}	
42.	Jakob von Oldensell	}	
43.	Johann Bispinck	}	
44.	Heinrich von Osnabrück	}	
45.	Hermann Kistemaker	}	
46.	Bernd Rulever	}	Responsible for the provision of beer and bread
47.	Johann Overdinck	}	
48.	Evert Roberg	}	Responsible for rampart construction
49.	Walter Kamphues	}	
50.	Bernd Busche		Coinsmith
51.	Hans Borstell		Goldsmith
52.	Gert von Düren		Sergeant of the main 'battle'
53.	Caspar Bornemann		Sergeant of the forlorn hope

LIST OF OFFICERS OF THE COURT AS DECREED BY JAN VON LEIDEN

54.	Kind von Oldensell }	Ensigns
55.	Johann von Jülich }	
56.	Schapp von Melven	Quartermaster of the main 'battle'[2]
57.	Spe	Quartermaster of the forlorn hope
58.	Arend von Oldenburg	Captain with the runners
59.	Adrian von Utrecht }	Gunners
60.	Gert von Schelve }	
61.	Heinrich von Xanten }	
62.	'lost child of Cologne' }	
63.	Urban Bilde }	
64.	Hans von der Langenstraße}	
65.	Bernd Wantscherer }	
66.	Jaspar Gelbgießer }	
67.	Evert Vollen	Fourrier
68.	Streveken	Officer in charge of the ramparts
69.	Rene }	Snipers
70.	Heinrich }	
71.	Tile }	
72.	Kort }	
73.	Scheferdt }	Skirmishers
74.	Bernd Olieschleger }	
75.	Otto Tilbecken Knecht }	
76.	Berendt Wichardes }	
77.	Peter Brunsinck }	
78.	Evert }	
79.	Heinrich von Lueck	Tailor
80.	Lübbert Haverhoven	Cook
81.	Dekeninck	Finance officer
82.	Friedrich Klinge	Butter churner
83.	Johann Schulte	Doorman
84.	Hermann Blad	Baker

---

2 *Gewalthaufen* – main column or 'battle' in an army.

'A MIGHTY FORTRESS OF GOD': THE SIEGE OF MÜNSTER 1534-35

85.	Lambert		Bailiff
86.	Windt		Barber
87.	Johan		Cooper
88.	Hermann Hagedorn,		Fisherman
89.	Johann Kuelmann,		Caretaker
90.	not specified		Fifer
91.	Hermann von Düren		Drummer
92.	Jaspar Weinschenke		Footman
93.	Christoph Waldeck		Page boy
94.	Hans Nepken	}	Keepers of the towers
95.	Johann tor Nate	}	
96.	Goswin Glasemaker	}	Envoys
97.	Hermann von Oldensell	}	
98.	Johann von dem Busche		Fireworker
99.	Hermann tor Nate		Cobbler
100.	Johann von Coesfeld		Saddler
101.	Johann von Darfeld	}	Smiths
102.	? Blasius	}	
103.	Wilhelm zum Turme		Glassmaker
104.	Johann Balke	}	Blacksmiths
105.	Der Stolte	}	
106.	Der Schwertfeger	}	
107.	? Roidtland	}	
108.	Hermann Reining	}	
109.	Klaus Scheiper	}	Masons
110.	Paul Notelis	}	
111.	? Berboem	}	
112.	Johann Edeler	}	
113.	Hermann Middendorp	}	
114.	Meister Hermann	}	
115.	? Evert	}	Carpenters
116.	Hermann Mackenborg	}	
117.	Schemme und Bernd Hinrekink }		

LIST OF OFFICERS OF THE COURT AS DECREED BY JAN VON LEIDEN

118.	? Gronover	}	Sappers responsible for the ramparts
119.	Bernd Travelmann	}	
118.	? Havickhorst	}	
121.	Botter Bernd	}	
122.	Paul Johan	}	

123. Ludger Ostermann — Organist

124.	Hermann in dem Slottel	}	Responsible for meat provision (*die fette Kost*).
125.	Johann Köninck	}	
126.	Hermann Reyning	}	Responsible for grain provisions
127.	Bernd Menneken	}	
128.	Ludecke Hoetmacker	}	Responsible for the distribution of clothing
129.	Johann Mordemann	}	
130.	Magnus Koheus	}	Responsible for procuring garments
131.	Klaus Stripe	}	
132.	Klaus Sneder	}	Responsible for distributing wood
133.	Heinrich Havickhorst	}	
134.	Johann Katerberg	}	Court orderlies
135.	Schulte von Legden	}	

The following women are to be the Queen and wives of the king

1. Divara von Haarlem
2. Maria Heckers
3. Katharina Milinges
4. Anna Laurentz
5. Angela Kerckerinck
6. Anna Averweges
7. Else Wantscherers
8. Else Dreiers
9. Anna Knipperdolling
10. Klara Knipperdolling
11. Katharina Averweges
12. Anna Kippenbroick

13. Christina Rodde
14. Margaretha Moderson
15. Lise von dem Busche
16. Grete Grolle

The Queen's Staff shall comprise:
1.	Heinrich Rodde	Chamberlain
2.	Peter Symesen	Head cook
3.	Johann von Soel	Doorkeeper
4.	Johann von Leiden	Treasurer
5.	Friedrich Insel	Wine server
6.	Engelbert Schenckinck	Tailor
7.	Andreas Koster	} Bodyguards
8.	Heinrich Wulff	}
9.	Heinrich Willenhues	Stoker
10.	Evert tor Heghe	Cook
11.	Sander von dem Busche	Lackey

Appendix IV

The Costs of the Siege

Accounts

Income

From Borrowings
- Bishop's own money   12,632 Gg.
- princes and private individuals lent   211,713 Gg.
- the nobility of the monastery gave   10,886 Gg.

subtotal: 235,231 Gg.

From public levies
- Territorial levies (7)   132,218 Gg.
- levy on the clergy   7,175 Gg.
- monasteries and cities   4,900 Gg.
- service payments from the Nobility   808 Gg.

subtotal: 145,101 Gg.

Total sum of the revenues: 380,332 Gg.

Expenditure
- Daily expenses   39,378 Gg.
- mercenaries and others   22,282 Gg.

                                                                          361,693 Eg.

- horsemen   638 Gg.
- and blockhouses   22,868 Eg.

• kitchen and messenger wages	434 Gg.
subtotal:	62,732 Gg
Subtotal of mercenary and blockhouse costs in Emden Guilders	384,561 Eg.*
combined	383,200 Gg
Not paid	9,216 Gg.
Total expenses:	392,416 Gg.

*Emden guilders (Eg) were valued at 25 against 30 gold guilders (Gg.) which accounts for the discrepancy in the conversion to gold guilders in the final tally.

The expenditure exceeds the income by 3,000 Gg., this sum probably came from the Bishop's booty, which he used to pay off his landsknechts. The actual cost of the war was, of course, far higher since some payments for material and labour were still outstanding and has been estimated at 500,000 gold guilders.[1]

---

1   Karl-Heinz Kirchhoff, 'Die Belagerung und Eroberung Münsters 1534/35' in *Westfälische Zeitschrift* volume 112 (1962), pp.146–147.

Appendix V

Glossary of Fortification Terms[1]

Scarp: the inner side of the ditch (closest to the curtain wall) is called the scarp (or escarp) slope. This may be revetted with masonry or brickwork, in which case, it is called the 'scarp wall'.
Cordon: a course of protruding masonry along the top of a scarp wall, intended to make it harder for an enemy to put a ladder against it.
Rampart: the actual wall of the fortress, which can be made of earth or masonry, is topped by a parapet for the defenders to fire over, and usually slopes away from the ditch (the 'exterior slope').
Berm: a ledge between the scarp wall and the exterior slope of the rampart, designed to increase the stability of the rampart and prevent any falling debris from compromising the ditch.
Faussebraye: a secondary parapet between the rampart and the inner edge of the ditch.
Carnot wall: a loopholed wall between the rampart and the inner edge of the ditch.
Chemin de Ronde: a pathway running along the berm, behind the faussebraye or carnot wall.
Cunette: a narrow channel that runs along the floor of the ditch for drainage purposes.
Bartardeau: a type of masonry dam across a ditch that is partly wet and partly dry.
Counterscarp: the outer slope or wall of the ditch (furthest from the fort).
Sally port: a small door allowing the defenders to enter the ditch should it be occupied by the enemy.
Caponier: a masonry or brick structure extending into the ditch or traversing across it; it would be pierced with loopholes to enable the defenders to fire along the floor of the ditch.

---

1 https://en.wikipedia.org/wiki/Ditch_(fortification) (accessed 17 September 2023).

'A MIGHTY FORTRESS OF GOD': THE SIEGE OF MÜNSTER 1534-35

Counterscarp Gallery: a passage constructed behind the counterscarp wall and pierced with loopholes, which enables the defenders to fire on attackers who have entered the ditch.

Glacis: an earth slope angled away from the ditch; the height and angle of the glacis was calculated to protect the rampart from direct fire but to allow the defenders to fire over it.

Covered Way: a path running between the outer edge of the ditch and the glacis, allowing defending troops to move around the exterior of the fort; it was usually provided with a banquette or fire step so that defenders could shoot over the crest of the glacis.

Place d'Armes (Place of Arms): an open area of the covered way at an angle of the ditch, where defenders could assemble for a sally or counterattack.

Bibliography

Published Books

Arthur, Anthony, *The Tailor-King: The Rise and Fall of the Anabaptist Kingdom of Muenster* (New York: St. Martin's Press, 1999)

Baumann, Reinhard, *Landsknechte* (Munich: C.H. Beck Verlag. 1994)

Burschell, Peter, *Söldner im Nordwestdeutschland des 16. und 17. Jahrhunderts* (Göttingen: Vandenhoeck & Ruprecht, 1994)

De Bakker, Willem, Driediger, Michael and Stayer, James, *Bernhard Rothmann and the Reformation in Münster, 1530-35* (Kitchener: Pandora Press, 2009)

Braunstein, Philippe, *Un banquier mis a nu: Autobiographie de Matthäus Schwarz, bourgeois d'Augsbourg* (Paris: Éditions Gallimard, 1992)

Cornelius, Carl Adolf, *Berichte der Augenzeugen uber das Münsterische Wiedertäuferreich* (London: Forgotten Books 2018 reprint)

Cornelius, Carl Adolf, *Die niederländischen Wiedertäufer während der Belagerung Münsters 1534 bis 1535* (Munich: Verlag der königlichen Akademie, 1869)

Drummond, Andrew, *The Dreadful History and Judgement of God on Thomas Müntzer* (London and New York: Verso, 2024)

Dülmen, Richard van, *Das Täuferreich zu Münster 1534-1535: Berichte und Dokumente* (Munich Deutscher Taschenbuch Verlag, 1974)

Johnson, Caroline, *The King's Servants: Men's dress at the accession of Henry VIII,* (Lightwater: Fat Goose Press Ltd, 2009)

Kerssenbroch, Hermann von (Christopher S. Mackay tr.), *Narratio Historica Anabaptistici Furoris Monasterium, Narrative of the Anabaptist Madness. The overthrow of Münster, the Famous Metropolis of Westphalia.* 2 volumes (Leiden–Boston: Brill 2007)

Kümper, Hiram, *Regimen Von der Wehrverfassung : Ein Kriegsmemorandum aus der Gießener Handschrift 996, zugleich ein Beitrag zur städtischen Militärgeschichte des 15. Jahrhunderts* (Berichte und Arbeiten aus der Universitätsbibliothek und dem Universitätsarchiv Gießen 55 2005)

Lipowec, Mathias, *Belagerungen in der frühen Neuzeit*. Diplomarbeit, Universität Wien. Historisch-Kulturwissenschaftliche Fakultät, 2013, http://othes.univie.ac.at/24770/ (accessed 2 February2022)

Mackay, Christopher, *False Prophets & Preachers: Henry Gresbeck's Account of the Anabaptist Kingdom of Münster*, (Kirksville: Truman State University Press, 2016)

Neumann Hartwig, *Festungsbau-Kunst und –Technik* (Bonn: Bernard & Graefe Verlag, 1994

Sattler, Joseph, *Die Wiedertäufer* (Berlin: Verlag J.A. Stargardt, 1895) http://amsterdamnified.ca/learn/reformations/media/joseph-sattler-die-wiedertufer-1895 (accessed 24 July 2023)

Stayer, James M. 1991, *The German Peasants' War and Anabaptist Community of Goods* (Montreal: McGill-Queen's University Press, 1991)

Tracy, James D., *Holland under Habsburg Rule 1506-1566: The Formation of a Body Politic* (Berkeley: University of California Press, 2018)

Rommé, Barbara (ed.), Der Zwinger. Bollwerk - Kunstwerk – Mahnmal (Münster: Aschendorff Verlag, 2007)

Waetzoldt, Wilhelm, *Dürers Befestigungslehre* (Berlin: J Bard, 1916)

Published Articles and Chapters

Eltis, David, 'Towns and Defence in Later Medieval Germany', *Nottingham Medieval Studies*: volume 33 (1989). https://deremilitari.org/2014/03/towns-and-defence-in-later-medieval-germany (accessed 7 July 2023).

Kirchhoff, Karl-Heinz, 'Die Belagerung und Eroberung Münsters 1534/35' in *Westfälische Zeitschrift* volume 112 (1962) pp.77–170

Kirchhoff, Karl-Heinz. 'Die Täufer im Münsterland Verbreitung und Verfolgung des Täufertums im Stift Münster 1533-1550' *Westfälische Zeitschrift - Zeitschrift für vaterländische Geschichte und Altertumskunde* 113 1963 pp.1–109 C:/Users/doug5/OneDrive/Documents/Siege%20of%20Muenster%20%20book/Kirchoff%20text%20aand%20transaltion/wz-9528.pdf (accessed 1 October 2023).

Klötzer, Ralf, 'The Melchiorites in Münster' in Stayer, James, Roth, John (Eds.) *A Companion to Anabaptism and Spiritualism, 1521–1700* (Leiden: Brill, 2006)

von der Lippe, George B., Reck-Malleczewen, Victoria M., Day of Wrath (Dies Irae). In: von der Lippe, G. B. & Reck-Malleczewen, V. M. (eds), *A History of the Münster Anabaptists* (New York: Palgrave Macmillan, 2008)

Landwehr, Achim, Fischer-Kattner, Anke, Hanß, Stefan, Lohsträter, Kai, Petersen, Sven, Schumann, Anja, *Militär und Zeit in der Frühen Neuzeit*, p.19 (Potsdam: Universitäts verlag Potsdam, 2017)

Militzer, Klaus, 'Die Bewaffnung der Bürger westdeutscher Städte im Spätmittelalter' in *Fasciculi Archaeologiae Historicae,* Fase. XI, 1998

Müller, Ernst (ed.), 'Die Abrechnung des Johannes Hageboke über die Kosten der Belagerung der Stadt Münster 1534-1535 Nebst der Abrechnung des Heinrich Flyncterinck über Büchsenmeister, Artillerie u. a.' in *Veröffentlichungen der Historischen Kommission des Provinzialinstituts für westfälische Landes- und Volkskunde III,* (Münster: Aschendorffsche Verlagsbuchhandlung, 1937)

Suderman, Henry, 'Sometimes it's the Place: the Anabaptist Kingdom Revisited' *Renaissance and Reformation*, volume 40 no.4, 2017, pp.117–140

Tippach, Thomas: Frühneuzeitliche Festungsstädte in Westfalen, in: Westfälischer Städteatlas, VI. Lieferung, hg. v. Wilfried Ehbrecht (Veröffentlichungen der Historischen Kommission für Westfalen, Altenbeken 1999)

Waite Gary K., 'The Anabaptist Movement in Amsterdam and the Netherlands, 1531-1535: An Initial Investigation into its Genesis and Social Dynamics' in *The Sixteenth Century Journal*, volume 18, no.2 (Summer, 1987), pp.249–265

Williamson Darren T., '"For the Honor Of God And To Fulfil His Will": The Role Of Polygamy in Anabaptist Münster' in *Restoration Quarterly*, Volume 1.1. 2000

Unpublished Theses

Mclaughlin, John M., 'Factors of Religious Violence And A Path To Peace: A Study of the 16th Century Anabaptists'. M.A. in Defence Analysis, Norwich University 2015

Nahmer, Ernst von der, 'Die *Wehrverfassungen der Deutschen* Städte in der zweiten Hälfte Des XIV Jahrhunderts'. Marburg Dissertation 1888

About the author

Doug Miller has been researching the military history of the first half of the 16th Century in Germany for over 40 years. He has authored Osprey titles on the Landsknechts, the Swiss and the Peasant Armies at the time of the German Reformation. He has published a study of the *Battle of Frankenhausen 1525* and authored the *Army of the Swabian League in 1525* and the *German Peasants' War* in this series. He is a member of the Association of German Peasants' War museums for which he continues to produce dioramas depicting specific episodes from the war. He lives in Newcastle upon Tyne, UK. This is his third book for Helion and Company.

About the artist

Giorgio Albertini was born in 1968 in Milan where he still lives. After studying Medieval History at the University of Milan, he become involved in archaeology and has been involved in several excavations for European institutions. He was responsible for the graphic depiction of archaeological sites and finds. He also works as a historical and scientific illustrator for many institutions, museums, and magazines such as *National Geographic Magazine, BBC History,* and *Medieval Warfare*. He has always been interested in military history and is one of the founders of *Focus Wars* magazine.

Other titles in the From Retinue to Regiment series:

No 1 *Richard III and the Battle of Bosworth* Mike Ingram

No 2 *Tanaka 1587: Japan's Greatest Unknown Samurai Battle* Stephen Turnbull

No 3 *The Army of the Swabian League 1525* Doug Miller

No 4 *The Italian Wars Volume 1: The Expedition of Charles VIII into Italy and the Battle of Fornovo* Massimo Predonzani & Alberici Vincenzo, translated by Irene Maccolini

No 5 *The Commotion Time: Tudor Rebellion in the West, 1549* E.T. Fox

No 6 *The Italian Wars Volume 2: Agnadello 1509, Ravenna 1512, Marignano 1515* Massimo Predonzani & Alberici Vincenzo, translated by Rachele Tiso

No 7 *The Tudor Arte of Warre Volume 1: The Conduct of War from Henry VII to Mary I, 1485-1558* Jonathan Davies

No 8 *The Ethiopian-Adal War 1529-1543: The Conquest of Abyssinia* Jeffrey M. Shaw

No 9 *The Ōnin War: A Turning Point in Samurai History* Stephen Turnbull

No 10 *One Faith, One Law, One King: French Armies of the Wars of Religion 1562–1598* T J O'Brien de Clare

No 11 *The Italian Wars Volume 3: Francis I and the Battle of Pavia 1525* Massimo Predonzani & Alberici Vincenzo

No 12 *On the Borderlands of Great Empires: Transylvanian Armies 1541-1613* Florin Nicolae Ardelean

No 14 *The Art of Shooting Great Ordnance: A History of the Development, Manufacture and Use of Artillery, 1494–1628* Jonathan Davies

No 15 *The Italian Wars Volume 4: The Battle of Ceresole 1544 - The Crushing Defeat of the Imperial Army* Massimo Predonzani & Simon Miller

No 16 *The Men of Warre: The Clothes, Weapons and Accoutrements of the Scots at War 1460–1600* Jenn Scott

No 17 *The German Peasants' War 1524-26* Douglas Miller

No 18 *The Tudor Arte of Warre Volume 2: The conduct of war in the reign of Elizabeth I, 1558–1603: Diplomacy, Strategy, Campaigns and Battles* Jonathan Davies

No 19 *The Kalmar War 1611–1613: Gustavus Adolphus's First War* Michael Fredholm von Essen

No 20 *Hojo: Samurai Warlords 1487–1590* Stephen Turnbull

No 21 *The Battle of Castillon 1453: The Death Knell for English France* Peter Hoskins

No 22 *The Tudor Arte of Warre Volume 3: The Conduct of War in the Reign of Elizabeth I 1558-1603: The Elizabethan Army* Jonathan Davies

No 23 *Sweden's War in Muscovy 1609-1617: The Relief of Moscow and Conquest of Novgorod* Michael Fredholm von Essen

No 24 *'Of Kerns and Gallowglasses': Irish Armies of the Sixteenth Century, 1487-1587* Robert Gresh

No 25 *'The Italian Wars Volume 5: The Franco-Spanish War in Southern Italy 1502-1504* Massimo Predonzani

No 26 *The Sieges of Rhodes 1480 and 1522* Jonathan Davies

No 27 *The Swabian War of 1499: The first confrontation between Landsknechts and the Swiss* Albert Winkler

No 28 *'A Mighty Fortress of God': The Siege of Münster 1534-35* Doug Miller